GRADE 6

McGraw-Hill's
Math

Mc
Graw
Hill

New York   Chicago   San Francisco   Lisbon   London   Madrid   Mexico City
Milan   New Delhi   San Juan   Seoul   Singapore   Sydney   Toronto

The **McGraw·Hill** Companies

Copyright © 2011 by the McGraw-Hill Companies, Inc. All rights reserved. Printed in the
United States of America. Except as permitted under the United States Copyright Act of
1976, no part of this publication may be reproduced or distributed in any form or by any
means, or stored in a database or retrieval system, without the prior written permission
of the publisher.

2 3 4 5 6 7 8 9 10 11 12 13 14 15 DOW/DOW 1 9 8 7 6 5 4 3 2

ISBN   978-0-07-174730-1
MHID   0-07-174730-3

Editorial Services: SkyBridge Publishing
Production Services: Watch This Space, Inc.
Design Services: PlanetGraham Design

Printed and bound by RR Donnelley

Cataloging-in-Publication data for this title are on file at the Library of Congress.

McGraw-Hill books are available at special quantity discounts for use as premiums and
sales promotions, or for use in corporate training programs. To contact a representative
please e-mail us at bulksales@mcgraw-hill.com.

This book is printed on acid-free paper.

Table of Contents

Table of Contents

To the Student

This book is designed to help you succeed in your sixth grade mathematics study. Short lessons explain key points, while exercises help you practice what you learned.

First, begin with the **Pretest**. This will identify areas that you need additional help with, as well as areas in which you are more comfortable.

Second, read the **Table of Contents**. Seeing how a book is organized will help guide your work.

Third, look at the **10-Week Summer Study Plan**. This will help you plan your time spent in practicing the skills you will master in this book. Remember, the Summer Study Plan is only a guide for you. You may proceed more quickly on some lessons, and you may need to spend more time on other lessons.

Fourth, notice the hints included in some of the lessons following the special **Remember** feature. These will help you remember key points that often make your mathematics work easier.

Fifth, take the **Posttest**. This test will demonstrate what you mastered as well as areas you may have to return to.

Finally, remember the old saying, "Practice makes perfect." In mathematics, practice may not guarantee perfection, but it certainly makes learning easier.

10-Week Summer Study Plan

Many students will use this book as a summer study program. If that's what you are doing, here is a handy 10-week study plan that can help you make the best use of your time.

When you complete each day's assignment, check it off by marking the box. Each assignment should take you approximately 30 minutes.

	Day	Lesson(s)	Test	✔
Week 1	Monday	1.1, 1.2	Pretest	
	Tuesday	1.3		
	Wednesday	2.1, 2.2		
	Thursday	3.1		
	Friday	3.2	Lessons 1–3 Unit Test	
Week 2	Monday	4.1, 4.2, 4.3		
	Tuesday	4.4, 4.5, 4.6		
	Wednesday	4.7, 4.8		
	Thursday	5.1, 5.2		
	Friday	5.3		
Week 3	Monday	6.1, 6.2		
	Tuesday	6.3, 6.4		
	Wednesday	7.1, 7.2		
	Thursday	7.3		
	Friday	7.4	Lessons 4–7 Unit Test	
Week 4	Monday	8.1, 8.2		
	Tuesday	8.3, 8.4		
	Wednesday	9.1, 9.2		
	Thursday	9.3, 9.4		
	Friday	10.1, 10.2, 10.3		
Week 5	Monday	11.1, 11.2		
	Tuesday	11.3, 11.4		
	Wednesday	11.5		
	Thursday	12.1, 12.2		
	Friday	12.3, 12.4	Lessons 8–12 Unit Test	

	Day	Lesson(s)	Test	✔
Week 6	Monday	13.1, 13.2		
	Tuesday	14.1		
	Wednesday	14.2		
	Thursday	14.3		
	Friday	14.4		
Week 7	Monday	15.1		
	Tuesday	15.2		
	Wednesday	15.3		
	Thursday	16.1, 16.2		
	Friday	16.3	Lessons 13–16 Unit Test	
Week 8	Monday	17.1, 17.2, 17.3, 17.4		
	Tuesday	17.5, 17.6, 17.7, 17.8		
	Wednesday	18.1, 18.2		
	Thursday	18.3, 18.4		
	Friday	19.1, 19.2	Lessons 17–19 Unit Test	
Week 9	Monday	20.1, 20.2		
	Tuesday	21.1, 21.2		
	Wednesday	22.1, 22.2, 22.3		
	Thursday	22.4		
	Friday	22.5	Lessons 20–22 Unit Test	
Week 10	Monday	23.1, 23.2		
	Tuesday	23.3, 23.4		
	Wednesday	24.1, 24.2, 24.3		
	Thursday	24.4, 24.5		
	Friday	24.6	Lessons 22–24 Unit Test & Posttest	

Pretest

Complete the follownng test items.

1 The Mayor of Tampa told Angela that there are three hundred thousand, six hundred, thirty five people living in their city. When she writes this number in standard form, Angela will write _____

2 Yousef is collecting signatures to build a park in his town. He needs 8,000 signatures to submit his petition. So far he has collected 2,875. Rounding to the nearest thousand, how many signatures can we estimate Yousef still needs to collect? _____

Calculate.

3
$$\begin{array}{r} 48 \\ \times\ 19 \\ \hline \end{array}$$

4
$$\begin{array}{r} 15 \\ \times\ 55 \\ \hline \end{array}$$

5
$$\begin{array}{r} 66 \\ \times\ 39 \\ \hline \end{array}$$

6
$$\begin{array}{r} 44 \\ \times\ 83 \\ \hline \end{array}$$

7 Miguel bought 11 cheese pizzas for his math club at school, but the club members only ate half of each pizza. How would Miguel express the amount of remaining pizza as an improper fraction? How would Miguel express the amount of remaining pizza as a mixed number? _____

Calculate.

8
$$\begin{array}{r} \$33.25 \\ \$27.50 \\ +\ \$16.15 \\ \hline \end{array}$$

9
$$\begin{array}{r} \$99.45 \\ -\ \$22.47 \\ \hline \end{array}$$

10
$$\begin{array}{r} \$2.99 \\ +\ \$3.02 \\ \hline \end{array}$$

11
$$\begin{array}{r} \$49.53 \\ +\ \$50.97 \\ \hline \end{array}$$

12 George has been measuring the amount of rainfall for the last three months. He measured 3.562 inches in April, 2.765 inches in May, and 3.015 inches in June. Rounding to the nearest tenth of an inch, what was the total amount of rainfall during these three months? _____

Calculate.

13 $78\overline{)1951}$

14 $34\overline{)625}$

15 $16\overline{)77}$

16 $11\overline{)145}$

17 Kaleigh is mixing paint for art class. The directions call for her to mix 17.25 milliliters of blue paint and 13.45 milliliters of yellow paint to achieve the right shade of green for her assignment. How much blue paint and how much yellow paint will she need in order to mix the right amount of paint for herself and two other classmates? _____

About how much green paint will she be making, altogether, for the three of them? _____

18 What is 60% of 120? _____

19 What is 40% of $\frac{3}{4}$? Express the number in both decimal and fraction form.

_____

20 Terrence has a length of rope that is $14\frac{3}{4}$ meters long. Forty percent of the rope's length is covered by a plastic film that makes it waterproof. What length of the rope is not waterproof? _____

21 Put the following decimals in order from least to greatest:
.0234, .05, .0001, .45, .019, .8, .0016, 1.076, .0978, .11

_____

22 Maynard bought a scale that records weight digitally. His math book weighs 2 kilograms, his science workbook weighs $\frac{3}{4}$ of a kilogram, his social studies book weighs $1\frac{1}{3}$ kilograms, and his language arts book weighs $3\frac{1}{2}$ kilograms. What is the total weight of the four books, in kilograms? _____

If a student is only allowed to carry 12.25 kilograms of books, will Maynard's four books exceed the limit? _____

What if Maynard removes the science workbook and adds a 3.75-kilogram dictionary? _____

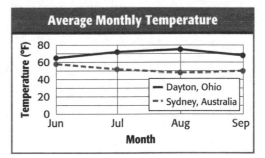

23 The chart shows how much time Nick and Laura spent last week listening to their favorite music. On which day did Laura listen to 90 minutes of music?

_____

On which day did Nick listen to music 85 minutes longer than Laura?

_____

24 Which city is colder in June?

During which month is the difference in temperature the greatest?

_____

25 Travis is looking at a solid figure that has a circular base, with curved sides that meet at a single point. What shape is he looking at?

_____

26 Fiona puts three small oranges, two apples, five pears, and ten carrots into a basket. What is the probability that if she reaches into the basket that she will pick a fruit? _____

27 Which of the following triangles is

obtuse? _____

right? _____

acute? _____

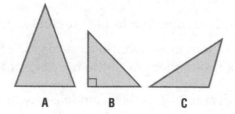

A   B   C

28 Calculate the following expression: $5 + (7 - 4)^2 + 4(3 + 2) - 6(2) =$ _____

29 Write the following number using scientific notation: 1,678,483.0043.

_____

30 Leslie collects teacups and saucers. Her collection consists of 3 teacups and 2 saucers from England, 2 teacups and 4 saucers from France, and 3 teacups from Japan. If each teacup costs $9 and each saucer costs $7, how much did Leslie spend for her collection? _____

31 Which of the following angles is

acute? _____

right? _____

obtuse? _____

123°   90°   55°

C   D   E

32 $32 \div .25 =$ _____

33 $.2505 \div .05 =$ _____

34 What is $\frac{24}{35} \div 6$?

_____

35 What is $16 \div \frac{8}{17}$?

_____

36 What is $\frac{32}{57} \div \frac{16}{19}$?

_____

Pretest

37 Harry is distributing rations for the class hike to the nature conservancy. Each student will carry $\frac{3}{4}$ liters of water and $\frac{1}{3}$ pound of trail mix for consumption during the trip. If there are 24 students on the trip, how much water and trail mix should Harry bring to distribute?

_____

38 Last week Jonas spent $9\frac{1}{6}$ hours working on his homework over a period of $4\frac{2}{3}$ days. How many hours a day, on average, did Jonas spend on his homework? _____

39 What is the decimal form of $7\frac{7}{8}$?

_____

40 What is the fraction form of 1.2?

_____

41 Freda is making a batch of multi-grain bread for the school picnic. Each loaf requires $1\frac{1}{2}$ cups of flour and $\frac{3}{4}$ cups of water. If Freda makes 8 loaves of bread, how many cups of flour and how many cups of water will she use? _____

42 What is $\frac{1}{3}$ of 60%? _____

43 What is 40% of $\frac{3}{4}$

in decimal form? _____

in fraction form? _____

44 What is the perimeter and area of the figure?

Perimeter _____

Area _____

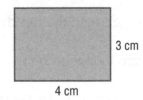

3 cm

4 cm

45 One inch is equivalent to 2.54 centimeters.

How many inches is 2.54 meters?

How many centimeters are in 100 inches?

_____ inches = 2.54 meters   100 inches = _____ centimeters

Name _____

Place Value

Place value tells you what each digit in a number means. The value of the digit depends on the place it occupies.

> **Example:** In the number 238, the 2 is in the hundreds place, the 3 is in the tens place and the 8 is in the ones place. So 238 means 2 hundreds + 3 tens + 8 ones.

USE A PLACE-VALUE CHART This place-value chart shows the places occupied by all the digits in the number 574,232,951.

Millions Period			Thousands Period			Ones Period		
Hundreds	Tens	Ones	Hundreds	Tens	Ones	Hundreds	Tens	Ones
5	7	4,	2	3	2,	9	5	1

In this number, the digit 5 is in the hundred millions place, the digit 7 is in the ten millions place, and so on.

DECIMAL PLACE VALUES Decimals have place values too. Look at this place-value chart.

Tens	Ones		Tenths	Hundredths	Thousandths
1	5	.	4	0	7

The number in the chart is 15.407. Read it like this: fifteen and four hundred seven thousandths.

NUMBER FORMS You can write a number in three different forms:

- **Standard form:** 4,368,129
- **Expanded form:** $(4 \times 1,000,000) + (3 \times 100,000) + (6 \times 10,000) + (8 \times 1,000) + (1 \times 100) + (2 \times 10) + (9 \times 1)$
- **Word form:** four million, three hundred sixty-eight thousand, one hundred twenty-nine

---

Exercises SOLVE

1. In 57,761, the underlined digit is in which place? _____

2. In 0.839, the number 8 is in which place? _____

3. In 8,730,562, which digit is in the hundreds place? _____

4. In 947,568,001, which digit is in the ten millions place? _____

5. The number 6 is in which place in 467,901,324? _____

6. Write the following in word form: 6,782,121 _____

7. In which place is the number 7 in 535,603.274? _____

8. The standard form of the number 458,905.43 has the number 9 in which place? _____

9. Which digit is in the hundredths place in the following number: 9,873,100.194? _____

10. In 9,640,862, the 8 is in what place? _____

11 Standard Form: 303,201.321

Expanded Form: _____

_____

Word Form: _____

_____

12 Standard Form: _____

Expanded Form: $(7 \times 100,000) + (3 \times 10,000) + (2 \times 1,000) + (9 \times 100) + (9 \times 10) + (8 \times 1) + (2 \times .1) + (7 \times .001)$

Word Form: _____

_____

13 Standard Form: _____

Expanded Form: _____

_____

Word Form: Twelve million, four hundred fifty-four thousand, seven hundred twenty one and ninety-six thousandths

14 Standard Form: _____

Expanded Form: $(4 \times 1,000,000) + (6 \times 10,000) + (3 \times 1,000) + (5 \times 100) + (2 \times .1) + (7 \times .001)$

Word Form: _____

_____

15 Standard Form: 1,559,461.625

Expanded Form: _____

_____

Word Form: _____

_____

16 Standard Form: _____

Expanded Form: _____

_____

Word Form: Four hundred forty-four thousand, two hundred thirty six and fifty-six thousandths

17 Nadine was watching her mom fill out a check to pay the electric bill. On the check she is required to write the amount of the check in standard form and in word form. Nadine's mother wrote a check for $1,396. What is that in word form? _____

_____

Name _____

Adding and Subtracting Whole Numbers

A **whole number** is a number that does not include any fractions or decimals. To add or subtract whole numbers, follow the steps shown below.

ADDING To add a group of whole numbers, line them up by place value. Add each place value separately, starting on the right. If the numbers in a column add up to a 2-digit number, "**carry**" the first digit over to the next column on the left. Look at the following example.

Example:

```
    2 1 ◄── The small numbers in
   254      the top row represent
    70      numbers that are carried.
 + 1389
 ───────
   1713
```

> **Remember...**
>
> When you are adding, don't worry about how many numbers you start with—or how large they are. Line up the numbers by place value. Then work on one place-value column at a time. Use "carrying" whenever a column adds up to a number greater than 9.

SUBTRACTING To subtract one whole number from another, line the numbers up by place value. Subtract each number separately beginning from the right. In the example below, how do you subtract 9 ones from 8 ones? The answer is by "**regrouping**." You reach into the tens column of 458 and take 1 ten. You regroup that 1 ten with the 8 in the ones column to make 18. Then subtract 9. But remember that there are now only 4 tens in the tens column of 458, not 5. Now subtract the number in the tens column. Finally, subtract the number in the hundreds column. In this example, the answer is 209.

Example:

```
   4 1 8 ◄── The small numbers in
   4̶5̶8̶      the top row represent
 − 249       "regrouping."
 ───────
   209
```

Exercises   ADD

1
```
  10901
 +  545
```

2
```
   555
  6666
 +  22
```

3
```
   12
    4
 + 87
```

4
```
   324
  4545
 +   1
```

5
```
  1212
    23
 + 2323
```

6
```
    65
    10
 + 2374
```

7
```
   127
   528
 +   5
```

8
```
   389
 28456
    21
 +   2
```

9
```
      2
     45
   3445
 + 1000
```

10
```
   8009
    909
 + 1090
```

11
```
    490
     32
     23
 +  101
```

12
```
     33
    333
   3333
 +    1
```

13
```
    544
    322
 + 1023
```

14
```
   1010
     11
 +  311
```

15
```
    212
    355
 +   22
```

16
```
      5
   1055
 +  454
```

17
```
     48
     49
 +  761
```

18
```
     34
    344
 +   43
```

19
```
     44
    555
 +   11
```

20
```
     10
     11
     12
     13
     15
 +  111
```

Exercises SUBTRACT

1
```
     22
 −    7
```

2
```
     72
 −   45
```

3
```
     43
 −   28
```

4
```
    555
 −  457
```

5
```
   4442
 − 3333
```

6
```
   2001
 −  999
```

7
```
   5888
 −  790
```

8
```
  10000
 − 8888
```

9
```
    878
 −  792
```

10
```
    313
 −  175
```

11
```
    888
 −  871
```

12
```
  12112
 − 9325
```

13
```
  15000
 − 12221
```

14
```
    767
 −  676
```

15
```
   1689
 − 1592
```

16
```
   2010
 − 1112
```

17
```
   1001
 −  988
```

18
```
   7443
 − 4567
```

19
```
    229
 −   49
```

20
```
   1811
 − 1729
```

Estimating Sums and Differences

To estimate sums and differences of whole numbers, begin by **rounding** each number. Rounding tells you *approximately* what the number is. To round, look at the highest place value in each number. That's called the rounding place. Then look at the second highest place value. If that is less than 5, keep the original digit in the rounding place. If the second highest place value is 5 or more, add 1 to the digit in the rounding place. When you have decided what digit should go in the rounding place, substitute 0 for *all* the other digits in the original number.

rounding place ⌐↓↓⌐ second highest place value

Example:

$$5481 \qquad 5000$$
$$+\ 2733 \qquad +\ 3000$$
$$\overline{} \qquad \overline{8000}$$

Remember...

When you estimate, your answer will not be exact. But it will probably be much better than a guess.

Exercises ESTIMATE

1 54 + 21

2 1124 − 555

3 3 + 44

4 5 + 29

5 44 + 46

6 670 + 650

7 67 − 33

8 655 − 211

9 431 − 251

10 1110 + 250

11 645 + 655

12 533 + 566

13 133 + 5675

14 1333 + 56750

15 677 − 532

16 444 + 555

17 1267 + 3487

18 21111 − 14750

19 4545 + 5459

20 750 − 449

Multiplying Whole Numbers

When you multiply whole numbers, start by lining up the numbers correctly. It is easy to line the numbers up if you're multiplying by a 1-digit number.

Example: Line up 593 × 7 this way

$$\begin{array}{r} {}^{6\,2} \\ 593 \\ \times\ \ \ 7 \\ \hline 4151 \end{array}$$

Multiply the 3 in the first line by the 7 in the second line. 3 × 7 = 21. You cannot write 21 in the ones place, so you do just what you did when adding. You write the 1 and save the 2 for the tens place. Keep that 2 in mind. Go back to the first line, and move one digit *to the left* to

multiply 9 × 7 = 63. Then you are ready to add that 2. You get 63 + 2 = 65. Write the 5 and set the 6 aside. Now go back to the first line again, and move one more digit to the left. Multiply 5 × 7 = 35. But remember the 6 you set aside. So 35 + 6 = 41. The **product**, or answer to this multiplication problem, is 4,151.

When you are multiplying a number by a 2-digit or 3-digit number, you have to be careful to line up the place values correctly.

Remember...

Always multiply the entire top number by just one bottom digit at a time. Use a different line for the product of each bottom digit.

Exercises **MULTIPLY**

1.
$$\begin{array}{r} 12 \\ \times\ 11 \\ \hline \end{array}$$

2.
$$\begin{array}{r} 15 \\ \times\ 16 \\ \hline \end{array}$$

3.
$$\begin{array}{r} 12 \\ \times\ 19 \\ \hline \end{array}$$

4.
$$\begin{array}{r} 22 \\ \times\ 7 \\ \hline \end{array}$$

5.
$$\begin{array}{r} 34 \\ \times\ 18 \\ \hline \end{array}$$

6.
$$\begin{array}{r} 45 \\ \times\ 31 \\ \hline \end{array}$$

7.
$$\begin{array}{r} 175 \\ \times\ 27 \\ \hline \end{array}$$

8.
$$\begin{array}{r} 345 \\ \times\ 76 \\ \hline \end{array}$$

9.
$$\begin{array}{r} 987 \\ \times\ 638 \\ \hline \end{array}$$

10.
$$\begin{array}{r} 27 \\ \times\ 36 \\ \hline \end{array}$$

11.
$$\begin{array}{r} 42 \\ \times\ 8 \\ \hline \end{array}$$

12.
$$\begin{array}{r} 286 \\ \times\ 354 \\ \hline \end{array}$$

13 777
      × 15

14 21
      × 22

15 928
      × 5

16 290
      × 11

17   12
       × 45

18 132
      × 34

19 111
      × 83

20 7895
      × 26

21   12
       × 677

22 384
      × 45

23 41
      × 44

24   65
       × 781

25   36
       × 35

26 854
      × 23

27 31
      × 21

28   44
       × 41

29 A grocery store received an order for 50 bags of apples. 15 apples can fit into each bag. How many apples will the grocery store need to fill the bags?

_____

30 Kerry is organizing his baseball cards into large envelopes. He can place 100 cards in each envelope. Kerry can fill 16 envelopes. How many baseball cards are in his collection?

_____

Estimating Products

To estimate products, begin by rounding. Then multiply the two rounded numbers.

> **Example:** Estimate 73 × 49
>
> **Step 1:** Round 73 *downward* to 70 and round 49 *upward* to 50.
>
> **Step 2:** Multiply 70 × 50

When multiplying two numbers that both end in zero, start by ignoring the final zeros. To multiply 70 × 50, just multiply 7 × 5 = 35.

After you have done that, restore all the zeros that you ignored to the right side of the product. **70 × 50 = 3500.**

Remember...

When you round both numbers *downward*, you know your estimate is *less* than the actual product. If you round both numbers *upward*, your estimate will be *more* than the actual product.

Exercises   ESTIMATE

1 44 × 12

2 87 × 85

3 13 × 12

4 545 × 737

5 97 × 147

6 234 × 901

7 67 × 33

8 147 × 151

9 454 × 3111

10 792 × 44

11 55 × 57

12 234 × 432

13 5467 × 6667

14 727 × 24

15 14 × 16

16 846 × 922

17 7 × 597

18 638 × 27

19 457 × 949

20 1111 × 5555

Name _____

Dividing Whole Numbers

When you divide, you have to know which number is the **dividend** and which number is the **divisor**. The **dividend** is the number to be divided. The **divisor** is the number that goes into the dividend. The answer, called the **quotient**, is the number of times the divisor can go into the dividend. If there is something left over when you are finished, you call that the **remainder**.

Example: Set up 653 ÷ 3 this way.

quotient ⟶ 217 R2 ⟵ remainder
divisor ⟶ 3)653 ⟵ dividend
        6
       ___
        5
        3
       ___
        23
        21
       ___
        2

Begin by looking at the *highest* place value in the dividend, the digit on the *left* side. Can that number be divided by the divisor? In this case, the answer is yes. 6 ÷ 3 = 2. Put the 2 above the line as the beginning of the quotient. Since 2 × 3 = 6, place this 6 under the 6 in dividend.

Next, subtract: 6 − 6 = 0. Now carry down from the dividend the digit in the next place value, 5. Can 5 be evenly divided by 3? This time the answer is no, but there is one 3 in 5. So write 1 in the quotient, and subtract again. Keep repeating these steps until you get to the last digit in the dividend. How many times can 23 be divided by 3? 23 ÷ 3 = 7, with 2 left over. The 2 is the remainder.

Remember...

When dividing, always begin on the *left* side of the dividend.

Exercises   DIVIDE

1. 89)627

2. 14)341

3. 15)346

4. 36)2814

5. 12)182

6. 9)84

7. 96)7499

8. 18)22220

9. 38)17330

10. 55)23270

11. 5)3647

12. 82)1399

13 $45\overline{)6621}$ **14** $13\overline{)1111}$ **15** $14\overline{)257}$ **16** $7\overline{)456}$

17 $9\overline{)803}$ **18** $11\overline{)499}$ **19** $6\overline{)3332}$ **20** $7\overline{)85}$

21 $12\overline{)157}$ **22** $7\overline{)3944}$ **23** $4\overline{)1115}$ **24** $17\overline{)1517}$

25 $9\overline{)777}$ **26** $54\overline{)38460}$ **27** $45\overline{)3830}$ **28** $8\overline{)452}$

29 Post office workers are placing envelopes in boxes. Each worker can place 625 envelopes per day. How many days will it take one worker to place 2,500 envelopes?

_____

30 Mr. Romanski is making information packets for all his new students. Each packet is 19 pages long. If he uses 342 sheets of paper, how many new students are in his class?

_____

3.2

Estimating Quotients

When you estimate the quotient of a division problem, you *do not* round the numbers. Instead, you try to find **compatible numbers**.

These are numbers that you can work with easily in your head.

Example: Estimate 5831 ÷ 8

Step 1: Look at the first two digits in the dividend, 58. Can you divide that evenly by the divisor, 8? No.

Step 2: Think about multiplying by 8.
$8 \times 6 = 48$ $8 \times 7 = 56$ $8 \times 8 = 64$
Select the one that is closest to 58.
That is 56.

Step 3: Add zeros to the dividend as placeholders. In this example, the dividend has four place values, so you need to add 2 zeros. 56**00**

Step 4: Divide by 8.
$5600 \div 8 = 700$

Exercises   ESTIMATE

1 146 ÷ 12

2 244 ÷ 8

3 91 ÷ 9

4 399 ÷ 13

5 412 ÷ 25

6 1321 ÷ 13

7 447 ÷ 9

8 672 ÷ 33

9 441 ÷ 91

10 252 ÷ 23

11 49 ÷ 4

12 3211 ÷ 80

13 1247 ÷ 50

14 333 ÷ 16

15 564 ÷ 11

16 233 ÷ 20

17 889 ÷ 45

18 489 ÷ 24

19 77 ÷ 5

20 732 ÷ 9

Lessons 1–3

Add or Subtract.

1
```
  266
+  45
```

2
```
  447
+  58
```

3
```
  1285
+  288
```

4
```
  4339
+  567
```

5
```
  739
+ 473
```

6
```
  639089
+  13487
```

7
```
  887
−  49
```

8
```
  138
−  76
```

9
```
  1468
−  249
```

10
```
  6539
−  144
```

11
```
  5882
−  993
```

12
```
  943
− 564
```

13
```
   6234
+ 14788
```

14
```
  24573
+ 29358
```

15
```
  57722
+  8989
```

16
```
  80453
+ 70809
```

17
```
  12661
  44867
+  9059
```

18
```
  79255
   5828
+  4770
```

19
```
  487
− 294
```

20
```
  1765
−  376
```

21
```
  28735350
−    18472
```

22
```
  22908
− 11192
```

23
```
  93556
− 55690
```

24
```
  18172
− 11188
```

Name _____

Lessons 1–3

Multiply or Divide.

25)
$$\begin{array}{r} 68 \\ \times\ 9 \\ \hline \end{array}$$

26)
$$\begin{array}{r} 86 \\ \times\ 8 \\ \hline \end{array}$$

27)
$$\begin{array}{r} 764 \\ \times\ 5 \\ \hline \end{array}$$

28)
$$\begin{array}{r} 253 \\ \times\ 4 \\ \hline \end{array}$$

29)
$$\begin{array}{r} 645 \\ \times\ 6 \\ \hline \end{array}$$

30)
$$\begin{array}{r} 865 \\ \times\ 7 \\ \hline \end{array}$$

31) $9\overline{)78}$

32) $4\overline{)43}$

33) $6\overline{)85}$

34) $63\overline{)798}$

35) $26\overline{)651}$

36) $81\overline{)348}$

37)
$$\begin{array}{r} 618 \\ \times\ 94 \\ \hline \end{array}$$

38)
$$\begin{array}{r} 459 \\ \times\ 82 \\ \hline \end{array}$$

39)
$$\begin{array}{r} 7604 \\ \times\ 35 \\ \hline \end{array}$$

40)
$$\begin{array}{r} 97253 \\ \times\ 684 \\ \hline \end{array}$$

41)
$$\begin{array}{r} 3845 \\ \times\ 566 \\ \hline \end{array}$$

42)
$$\begin{array}{r} 78865 \\ \times\ 877 \\ \hline \end{array}$$

43) $28\overline{)588}$

44) $17\overline{)773}$

45) $46\overline{)285}$

46) $63\overline{)798}$

47) $36\overline{)43456}$

48) $81\overline{)63348}$

Lessons 1-3

49 Principal Haines is planning for the school's upcoming academic year. There are 335 students in Grade 6, 407 in Grade 7, and 298 in Grade 8. How many students are in Principal Haines's middle school?

_____

50 If Principal Haines wanted to lower the class size to 23 students in each

class, how many classes will she have in Grade 6? _____

Grade 7? _____   Grade 8? _____
(Count the remainder as another class.)

51 Last year Todd had 435 stamps in his stamp collection. This year Todd added 76 more. How many stamps does he have in his collection now?

_____

52 Eurydice's favorite book has 47 chapters. Each chapter averages 17 pages in length. About how many pages are in the book? _____

How many pages exactly? _____

53 At 1,622 feet in length, the Commodore John Barry Bridge in Philadelphia is one of the longest cantilevered bridges in the world. What is the length of the bridge written in word form?

_____

54 What is the expanded form of the number 7,456,932?

_____

_____

55 During the latest census, in 2000, the estimated population of the United States was two hundred seventy four million, nine hundred forty three thousand, four hundred ninety six. What is the standard form of that number?

_____

The results of the 2010 Census are expected to show an increase of 30,500,950 in the population estimate. What is the new estimated population of the United States written in standard form?

_____

In expanded form? _____

_____

4.1

Name _____

Changing Improper Fractions to Mixed Numbers

In a fraction, the number on the bottom is the **denominator**. The denominator tells what kind of units the whole is divided into. The number on the top is the **numerator**. It tells how many of those units there are.

When the numerator is the same as the denominator, a fraction is equal to 1. When the numerator is *greater* than the denominator, a fraction is equal to more than 1. This is called an **improper fraction**. Sometimes, it is easier to perform a calculation when you change an improper fraction into a **mixed number**, part whole number and part fraction. These are mixed numbers:

$$8\frac{3}{4}, \ 21\frac{1}{2}, \ 147\frac{5}{9}$$

To change an improper fraction to a mixed number, divide the numerator by the denominator. The quotient is the whole number part. If there is a remainder, that becomes the fraction part. Simply use the remainder as the numerator and keep the original denominator.

Example: Change $\frac{17}{5}$ to a mixed number.

Step 1: Divide the numerator by the denominator.
$17 \div 5 = 3$ R2

Step 2: The quotient becomes the whole number and the remainder becomes the fraction.
So $\frac{17}{5} = 3\frac{2}{5}$

Exercises   CHANGE TO MIXED NUMBERS

1. $\frac{22}{7}$
2. $\frac{35}{4}$
3. $\frac{73}{10}$
4. $\frac{47}{3}$
5. $\frac{87}{11}$

6. $\frac{35}{6}$
7. $\frac{26}{5}$
8. $\frac{111}{8}$
9. $\frac{32}{3}$
10. $\frac{66}{5}$

11. $\frac{211}{11}$
12. $\frac{21}{4}$
13. $\frac{78}{7}$
14. $\frac{82}{9}$
15. $\frac{13}{2}$

16. $\frac{67}{4}$
17. $\frac{11}{8}$
18. $\frac{43}{14}$
19. $\frac{137}{13}$
20. $\frac{45}{2}$

22   Lesson 4.1   Changing Improper Fractions to Mixed Numbers

Changing Mixed Numbers to Improper Fractions

To change mixed numbers into improper fractions, find the fraction part of the mixed number. Multiply the whole number by the denominator of the fraction. Then, add the numerator to that product and place the total over the denominator.

Example: Change $9\frac{7}{8}$ into an improper fraction.

Step 1: Multiply $9 \times 8 = 72$

Step 2: $72 + 7 = 79$

Step 3: $\frac{79}{8}$ So $9\frac{7}{8} = \frac{79}{8}$

Exercises   **CHANGE TO IMPROPER FRACTIONS**

1 $2\frac{2}{3}$ **2** $5\frac{4}{7}$ **3** $21\frac{3}{5}$ **4** $5\frac{3}{8}$ **5** $22\frac{6}{7}$

6 $15\frac{4}{11}$ **7** $13\frac{2}{3}$ **8** $3\frac{11}{17}$ **9** $2\frac{4}{19}$ **10** $6\frac{3}{4}$

11 $1\frac{1}{51}$ **12** $55\frac{1}{2}$ **13** $10\frac{2}{23}$ **14** $6\frac{4}{7}$ **15** $13\frac{2}{7}$

16 $42\frac{1}{3}$ **17** $5\frac{1}{19}$ **18** $12\frac{2}{3}$ **19** $2\frac{3}{4}$ **20** $200\frac{33}{100}$

Name _____

Adding Fractions with Like Denominators

Like denominators are exactly the same. For example, $\frac{1}{4}$ and $\frac{3}{4}$ have like denominators. But $\frac{1}{4}$ and $\frac{1}{2}$ do *not* have like denominators.

To add fractions with like denominators, just add the numerators. Place the total over the denominator.

You may notice that your total is an improper fraction. But you learned how to change that into a mixed number if you need to.

Remember...

Like denominators are the same, and are sometimes called common denominators.

Example: Add: $\frac{3}{7} + \frac{4}{7} + \frac{6}{7}$

Step 1: Add $3 + 4 + 6 = 13$

Step 2: Place the total over the like denominator. $\frac{13}{7}$

Exercises ADD FRACTIONS

1 $\frac{1}{2} + \frac{3}{2}$

2 $\frac{7}{3} + \frac{6}{3}$

3 $\frac{6}{11} + \frac{6}{11}$

4 $\frac{5}{19} + \frac{2}{19}$

5 $\frac{3}{7} + \frac{6}{7}$

6 $\frac{4}{3} + \frac{2}{3}$

7 $\frac{1}{5} + \frac{4}{5}$

8 $\frac{9}{33} + \frac{17}{33}$

9 $\frac{1}{10} + \frac{7}{10}$

10 $\frac{22}{37} + \frac{14}{37}$

11 $\frac{16}{97} + \frac{32}{97}$

12 $\frac{14}{23} + \frac{3}{23}$

13 $\frac{10}{13} + \frac{7}{13}$

14 $\frac{5}{9} + \frac{2}{9}$

15 $\frac{10}{39} + \frac{23}{39}$

16 $\frac{1}{4} + \frac{3}{4}$

17 $\frac{4}{14} + \frac{4}{14}$

18 $\frac{5}{7} + \frac{8}{7}$

Subtracting Fractions with Like Denominators

To subtract fractions with like denominators, look at the numerators. Place the difference over the like denominator.

Example: Subtract: $\frac{13}{25} - \frac{9}{25}$

Step 1: Subtract $13 - 9 = 4$

Step 2: Place the difference over the like denominator. $\frac{4}{25}$

Remember...

When adding or subtracting fractions with like denominators, just work with the numerators. You can *ignore* the like denominators while adding or subtracting. However, do not forget to put your total or difference over the like denominator when you have finished your calculations.

Exercises   SUBTRACT FRACTIONS

1 $\frac{5}{7} - \frac{2}{7}$

2 $\frac{11}{13} - \frac{7}{13}$

3 $\frac{10}{11} - \frac{9}{11}$

4 $\frac{13}{21} - \frac{8}{21}$

5 $\frac{2}{3} - \frac{1}{3}$

6 $\frac{10}{47} - \frac{10}{47}$

7 $\frac{43}{96} - \frac{18}{96}$

8 $\frac{12}{13} - \frac{11}{13}$

9 $\frac{47}{49} - \frac{32}{49}$

10 $\frac{43}{31} - \frac{23}{31}$

11 $\frac{5}{7} - \frac{2}{7}$

12 $\frac{10}{17} - \frac{7}{17}$

13 $\frac{3}{4} - \frac{2}{4}$

14 $\frac{14}{15} - \frac{4}{15}$

15 $\frac{7}{12} - \frac{5}{12}$

16 $\frac{6}{7} - \frac{2}{7}$

17 $\frac{7}{8} - \frac{5}{8}$

18 $\frac{5}{13} - \frac{2}{13}$

Name _____

Adding or Subtracting Fractions with Unlike Denominators

To add or subtract fractions with unlike, or different, denominators, you have to change them into fractions with common or like denominators. This process is called finding the **common denominator**.

Example: Add $\frac{3}{4} + \frac{2}{6} = \frac{9}{12} + \frac{4}{12} = \frac{13}{12} = 1\frac{1}{12}$

Subtract $\frac{3}{4} - \frac{2}{6} = \frac{9}{12} - \frac{4}{12} = \frac{5}{12}$

To find a common denominator in these fractions, first, look at the denominators, 4 and 6. What number is a multiple of both 4 and 6? A simple way to find the **common multiple** is to multiply the two numbers.

$4 \times 6 = 24$. In some cases, there is a smaller number that is a common multiple that would be easier to work with. In these examples, 12 is a lower common multiple than 24, so it will work as your common denominator. In each fraction, multiply the original denominator to make it become the common denominator. Then multiply the original numerator by that same number.

Exercises   ADD OR SUBTRACT

1 $\frac{2}{7} + \frac{3}{5}$

2 $\frac{4}{13} + \frac{2}{3}$

3 $\frac{3}{4} + \frac{1}{8}$

4 $\frac{3}{11} + \frac{2}{7}$

5 $\frac{2}{5} + \frac{3}{4}$

6 $\frac{2}{7} + \frac{1}{4}$

7 $\frac{2}{3} - \frac{1}{4}$

8 $\frac{5}{6} - \frac{1}{8}$

9 $\begin{array}{r} \frac{13}{15} \\ + \frac{2}{7} \\ \hline \end{array}$

10 $\begin{array}{r} \frac{12}{13} \\ - \frac{2}{3} \\ \hline \end{array}$

11 $\begin{array}{r} \frac{3}{4} \\ + \frac{1}{5} \\ \hline \end{array}$

12 $\begin{array}{r} \frac{3}{4} \\ - \frac{2}{5} \\ \hline \end{array}$

13 $\begin{array}{r} \frac{3}{4} \\ + \frac{1}{7} \\ \hline \end{array}$

14 $\begin{array}{r} \frac{1}{3} \\ - \frac{1}{4} \\ \hline \end{array}$

15 $\begin{array}{r} \frac{5}{11} \\ - \frac{2}{10} \\ \hline \end{array}$

16 $\begin{array}{r} \frac{3}{4} \\ - \frac{1}{16} \\ \hline \end{array}$

Name _____

Adding Mixed Numbers with Unlike Denominators

There are two ways to do this. You could change each mixed number to an improper fraction and then add them. But an easier way to add mixed numbers is to add the whole number parts first and then add the fractions.

Example: Add $2\frac{3}{5} + 5\frac{2}{3}$

Step 1: Add the whole numbers. $2 + 5 = 7$
Now add the fractions $\frac{3}{5} + \frac{2}{3}$

Step 2: Change the fractions with unlike denominators to fractions with a common denominator.
$$\frac{3 \times 3}{5 \times 3} = \frac{9}{15} \qquad \frac{2 \times 5}{3 \times 5} = \frac{10}{15}$$

Step 3: Add the fractions. $\frac{9}{15} + \frac{10}{15} = \frac{19}{15}$

Step 4: If the numerator in the total is greater than the common denominator, you have an improper fraction. Change it to a mixed number. $\frac{19}{15} = 1\frac{4}{15}$

Step 5: Add your two totals.
$$7 + 1\frac{4}{15} = 8\frac{4}{15}$$

Exercises   ADD

1 $1\frac{2}{3} + 3\frac{1}{5}$

2 $4\frac{1}{7} + 3\frac{3}{5}$

3 $5\frac{1}{9} + 2\frac{3}{7}$

4 $1\frac{2}{3} + 4\frac{1}{16}$

5 $10\frac{3}{7} + 2\frac{3}{11}$

6 $3\frac{1}{4} + 5\frac{2}{9}$

7 $11\frac{2}{7} + 12\frac{3}{8}$

8 $12\frac{5}{6} + 1\frac{1}{15}$

9 $\begin{aligned} 13\frac{2}{7} \\ + 3\frac{2}{9} \\ \hline \end{aligned}$

10 $\begin{aligned} 21\frac{1}{9} \\ + 3\frac{5}{6} \\ \hline \end{aligned}$

11 $\begin{aligned} 2\frac{2}{3} \\ + 2\frac{2}{5} \\ \hline \end{aligned}$

12 $\begin{aligned} 3\frac{1}{5} \\ + 4\frac{5}{6} \\ \hline \end{aligned}$

13 $\begin{aligned} 3\frac{5}{9} \\ + 2\frac{3}{4} \\ \hline \end{aligned}$

14 $\begin{aligned} 5\frac{1}{2} \\ + 4\frac{1}{9} \\ \hline \end{aligned}$

15 $\begin{aligned} 4\frac{7}{8} \\ + 2\frac{2}{9} \\ \hline \end{aligned}$

16 $\begin{aligned} 3\frac{1}{2} \\ + 2\frac{2}{7} \\ \hline \end{aligned}$

Subtracting Mixed Numbers with Unlike Denominators

To subtract mixed numbers, first subtract the whole numbers, then subtract the fractions.

Example: Subtract $7\frac{3}{8} - 3\frac{1}{4}$

Step 1: $7 - 3 = 4$

Step 2: Change the fractions with unlike denominators to fractions with a common denominator. The lowest common multiple of 8 and 4, is 8. In this case $4 \times 2 = 8$. The best common multiple is the *higher* number.

Step 3: Subtract the fractions. $\frac{3}{8} - \frac{2}{8} = \frac{1}{8}$

Step 4: Add your two differences.
$$4 + \frac{1}{8} = 4\frac{1}{8}$$

Exercises   SUBTRACT

1 $2\frac{5}{8} - 1\frac{1}{4}$

2 $4\frac{6}{7} - 2\frac{3}{4}$

3 $5\frac{4}{9} - 2\frac{1}{3}$

4 $7\frac{7}{8} - 5\frac{1}{5}$

5 $2\frac{1}{10} - 1\frac{1}{11}$

6 $5\frac{3}{4} - 4\frac{2}{3}$

7 $7\frac{7}{9} - 2\frac{1}{4}$

8 $5\frac{3}{7} - 2\frac{1}{6}$

9 $\begin{array}{r} 5\frac{1}{4} \\ -\ 2\frac{2}{13} \\ \hline \end{array}$

10 $\begin{array}{r} 19\frac{6}{7} \\ -\ 3\frac{3}{10} \\ \hline \end{array}$

11 $\begin{array}{r} 4\frac{2}{3} \\ -\ 1\frac{1}{8} \\ \hline \end{array}$

12 $\begin{array}{r} 10\frac{7}{10} \\ -\ 7\frac{5}{9} \\ \hline \end{array}$

13 Mario is selling lemonade to raise money for his school. He started with $8\frac{1}{2}$ gallons of lemonade and has, so far, sold $3\frac{7}{8}$ gallons. How many gallons does he have left to sell?

_____

14 Bethany is making strawberry shortcake for her entire family. The recipe calls for $1\frac{3}{5}$ pounds of strawberries. If Bethany purchases $1\frac{7}{8}$ pounds, but drops $\frac{1}{4}$ pound of strawberries on her way home, will she have enough to complete the recipe?

_____

Estimating Sums and Differences of Fractions and Mixed Numbers

FRACTIONS When you add or subtract fractions, ask: Is each fraction closest to 0, to $\frac{1}{2}$, or to 1?

Example: Estimate $\frac{2}{5} + \frac{8}{9} + \frac{1}{8}$

Step 1: $\frac{2}{5}$ is a little bit less than $\frac{1}{2}$.

$\frac{8}{9}$ is very close to 1.

$\frac{1}{8}$ is not much more than 0.

Step 2: Add: $\frac{1}{2} + 1 + 0 = 1\frac{1}{2}$

MIXED NUMBERS To estimate mixed numbers when you are adding, start by estimating the total of the whole numbers. Then estimate the total of the fractions. Add your two estimates together. See the subtraction example.

Example: Estimate $51\frac{15}{16} - 39\frac{4}{7}$

Step 1: Estimate the difference of the whole numbers.
$51 - 39$ can be rounded to
$50 - 40 = 10$.

Step 2: Then estimate the difference of the fractions. $\frac{15}{16}$ is almost 1.
$\frac{4}{7}$ is slightly more than $\frac{1}{2}$. $1 - \frac{1}{2} = \frac{1}{2}$

Step 3: Add the two differences. A good estimate would be $10 + \frac{1}{2} = 10\frac{1}{2}$

Exercises   ESTIMATE

1 $\frac{3}{4} + \frac{5}{6}$

2 $\frac{4}{5} + \frac{1}{7}$

3 $\frac{1}{3} + \frac{4}{7}$

4 $\frac{5}{6} + \frac{4}{8}$

5 $1\frac{1}{5} + 2\frac{5}{6}$

6 $7\frac{4}{5} + 4\frac{1}{3}$

7 $5\frac{1}{5} - 2\frac{3}{5}$

8 $7\frac{1}{2} - \frac{3}{4}$

9 $12\frac{1}{8} + \frac{2}{3}$

10 $4\frac{4}{7} + 4\frac{4}{7}$

11 $13\frac{5}{8} - 12\frac{1}{4}$

12 $17\frac{1}{7} - 13\frac{3}{4}$

13 Leslie had $25\frac{4}{9}$ ounces of cat food left in a bag. If she feeds each of her two cats $1\frac{7}{8}$ ounces of food, about how much cat food will she have left?

_____

14 James was gathering wood for the fireplace. He already had $1\frac{4}{5}$ cords of wood and he gathered another $2\frac{1}{3}$ cords today. About how many cords of wood does James have now?

_____

Name _____

Multiplying Fractions and Whole Numbers

To multiply a fraction and a whole number, you need to multiply the *numerator* by the whole number. Then place the product over the denominator.

Example: Multiply $13 \times \frac{7}{8}$

Step 1: Multiply the whole number by the numerator of the fraction.
$13 \times 7 = 91$

Step 2: Place the product over the denominator of the original fraction. $\frac{91}{8}$

Step 3: The product will often be an improper fraction. You may need to change it to a mixed number.
$\frac{91}{8} = 11\frac{3}{8}$

Exercises MULTIPLY

1 $5 \times \frac{3}{4}$ **2** $4 \times \frac{2}{7}$ **3** $21 \times \frac{5}{8}$ **4** $11 \times \frac{2}{9}$ **5** $4 \times \frac{3}{11}$

6 $13 \times \frac{13}{14}$ **7** $21 \times \frac{10}{23}$ **8** $7 \times \frac{2}{3}$ **9** $12 \times \frac{7}{19}$ **10** $14 \times \frac{3}{5}$

11 $14 \times \frac{11}{3}$ **12** $13 \times \frac{4}{17}$ **13** $10 \times \frac{9}{23}$ **14** $13 \times \frac{21}{22}$ **15** $5 \times \frac{14}{27}$

16 Chet found a pair of sunglasses that he would like to buy. They normally cost $43.00, but this week they are on sale for only $\frac{7}{8}$ of the usual price. How much money will Chet need to buy the sunglasses?

_____

17 Ashlee is riding her bike to the beach. If the beach is 17 miles from her home, and she has already traveled $\frac{3}{5}$ of the way, how much farther does she have to cycle?

_____

Multiplying Fractions: Reciprocals

To multiply fractions, treat the numerators and the denominators as two different multiplication exercises. Multiply the numerators to find the numerator of the product. Then multiply the denominators to find the denominator of the product.

Example: $\frac{4}{5} \times \frac{3}{7}$

Step 1: Multiply the numerators.
$4 \times 3 = 12$

Step 2: Multiply the denominators.
$5 \times 7 = 35$

Step 3: Write the product. $\frac{12}{35}$

You may need to multiply **reciprocals**. Reciprocals are two fractions that look like upside-down reflections of one another. The numerator of the first is the denominator of the second and the numerator of the second is the denominator of the first.

Example: $\frac{2}{3} \times \frac{3}{2}$

You *could* go through the steps of multiplying the numerators ($2 \times 3 = 6$), and then multiplying the denominators ($3 \times 2 = 6$). Notice that the products are the same. When multiplying reciprocals, the product of the numerators and the product of the denominators will *always* be the same.

Remember...

To multiply fractions, multiply the numerators first, then the denominators.

Exercises MULTIPLY

1. $\frac{1}{2} \times \frac{1}{2}$
2. $\frac{2}{3} \times \frac{6}{7}$
3. $\frac{5}{9} \times \frac{3}{11}$
4. $\frac{10}{13} \times \frac{1}{3}$
5. $\frac{3}{11} \times \frac{11}{3}$

6. $\frac{7}{3} \times \frac{3}{11}$
7. $\frac{4}{5} \times \frac{7}{8}$
8. $\frac{3}{4} \times \frac{4}{3}$
9. $\frac{17}{27} \times \frac{5}{3}$
10. $\frac{6}{10} \times \frac{6}{11}$

11. $\frac{13}{14} \times \frac{2}{3}$
12. $\frac{4}{5} \times \frac{4}{5}$
13. $\frac{133}{145} \times \frac{145}{133}$
14. $\frac{8}{19} \times \frac{5}{7}$
15. $\frac{11}{13} \times \frac{9}{14}$

16. $\frac{32}{33} \times \frac{1}{2}$
17. $\frac{1}{5} \times \frac{1}{7}$
18. $\frac{5}{6} \times \frac{5}{9}$
19. $\frac{2}{3} \times \frac{33}{34}$
20. $\frac{45}{47} \times \frac{47}{45}$

Name _____

Multiplying Fractions and Mixed Numbers: Reducing

MULTIPLY FRACTIONS AND MIXED NUMBERS The easiest way to multiply fractions and mixed numbers is to change the mixed number into an improper fraction. Then multiply the fractions just as you normally would.

Example: Multiply: $3\frac{1}{2} \times \frac{4}{9}$

Step 1: Change the mixed number to an improper fraction. $3\frac{1}{2} = \frac{7}{2}$

Step 2: Restate the problem. $\frac{7}{2} \times \frac{4}{9}$

Step 3: Multiply the numerators. $7 \times 4 = 28$

Step 4: Multiply the denominators. $2 \times 9 = 18$

Step 5: Write the product. $\frac{28}{18}$

REDUCING You may already know about reducing a fraction. Reducing changes a fraction into its simplest form. For example: $\frac{3}{15} = \frac{1}{5}$. To reduce, see if you can divide *both* the numerator and the denominator by the *same* number. In this case, you were able to divide both 3 and 15 by 3.

When you have an improper fraction, you can reduce it. $\frac{28}{18} = \frac{14}{9}$ because you were able to divide both 28 and 18 by 2. You can also reduce the fraction part of a mixed number. $1\frac{10}{18} = 1\frac{5}{9}$ because both 10 and 18 are divisible by 2.

Remember...

When you reduce a mixed number, the whole number will *always* stay the same.

Exercises   MULTIPLY, REDUCE

1 $1\frac{1}{2} \times \frac{4}{5}$

2 $\frac{2}{9} \times 4\frac{1}{4}$

3 $\frac{3}{4} \times 2\frac{1}{7}$

4 $5\frac{1}{3} \times \frac{1}{2}$

5 $\frac{8}{9} \times 3\frac{1}{5}$

6 $1\frac{2}{3} \times \frac{2}{7}$

7 $5\frac{1}{4} \times \frac{2}{3}$

8 $7\frac{1}{8} \times \frac{1}{4}$

9 $1\frac{1}{2} \times \frac{8}{9}$

10 $\frac{3}{7} \times 5\frac{1}{7}$

11 $\frac{1}{3} \times 5\frac{2}{3}$

12 $\frac{5}{6} \times 1\frac{1}{5}$

13 $\frac{3}{4} \times 5\frac{1}{3}$

14 $3\frac{1}{4} \times \frac{3}{7}$

15 $5\frac{2}{11} \times \frac{22}{23}$

Multiplying Fractions and Mixed Numbers: Reducing (cont.)

MULTIPLY MIXED NUMBERS You can probably figure out the easiest way to multiply mixed numbers. Change them to improper fractions.

Example: Multiply: $4\frac{2}{3} \times 3\frac{3}{8}$

Step 1: Change the first mixed number to an improper fraction. $4\frac{2}{3} = \frac{14}{3}$

Step 2: Change the next mixed number to an improper fraction. $3\frac{3}{8} = \frac{27}{8}$

Step 3: Restate the problem. $\frac{14}{3} \times \frac{27}{8}$

Step 4: Multiply the numerators. $14 \times 27 = 378$

Step 5: Multiply the denominators. $3 \times 8 = 24$

Step 6: Write the product. $\frac{378}{24}$

Reduce the fraction, if you can. In this example, both 378 and 24 can be divided by 6. $\frac{378}{24} = \frac{63}{4}$

MORE ABOUT REDUCING Here is a good trick for reducing when you multiply two fractions. Look at both numerators and then at both denominators. If you can divide *either* of those numerators by the same number as *either* of the denominators, you can reduce!

Example: Multiply $\frac{14}{3} \times \frac{27}{8}$

The numerator 14 and the denominator 8 can both be divided by 2.

So $\frac{14}{3} \times \frac{27}{8} = \frac{7}{3} \times \frac{27}{4}$

Now, look again. The numerator 27 and the denominator 3 can both be divided by 3.

So $\frac{7}{3} \times \frac{27}{4} = \frac{7}{1} \times \frac{9}{4}$. Since $\frac{7}{1} = 7$, now you have a much simpler exercise to solve.

$7 \times \frac{9}{4} = \frac{63}{4}$

Exercises   MULTIPLY, REDUCE

1 $1\frac{1}{4} \times 2\frac{2}{3}$ **2** $2\frac{1}{5} \times 5\frac{1}{4}$ **3** $5\frac{1}{8} \times 2\frac{2}{3}$ **4** $2\frac{3}{7} \times 2\frac{3}{4}$ **5** $2\frac{1}{7} \times 1\frac{1}{3}$

6 $2\frac{1}{2} \times 3\frac{2}{3}$ **7** $3\frac{1}{3} \times 1\frac{2}{3}$ **8** $3\frac{4}{5} \times 1\frac{1}{2}$ **9** $3\frac{1}{2} \times 2\frac{1}{7}$ **10** $4\frac{3}{5} \times 2\frac{1}{3}$

11 $4\frac{1}{2} \times 3\frac{1}{3}$ **12** $5\frac{2}{3} \times 2\frac{1}{16}$ **13** $1\frac{1}{2} \times 1\frac{1}{8}$ **14** $3\frac{1}{4} \times 2\frac{3}{5}$ **15** $5\frac{1}{2} \times 1\frac{7}{8}$

Name _____

Dividing Fractions by Whole Numbers

To divide a fraction by a whole number, multiply the denominator of the fraction by the whole number.

Example: Divide: $\frac{5}{8} \div 2$

Step 1: Keep the original numerator.

Step 2: Multiply the denominator of the fraction by the whole number. $8 \times 2 = 16$. This is the new denominator.

So $\frac{5}{8} \div 2 = \frac{5}{16}$

Exercises DIVIDE

1 $\frac{1}{2} \div 4$

2 $\frac{3}{5} \div 4$

3 $\frac{6}{7} \div 3$

4 $\frac{1}{2} \div 6$

5 $\frac{5}{19} \div 2$

6 $\frac{4}{5} \div 7$

7 $\frac{1}{9} \div 9$

8 $\frac{3}{11} \div 12$

9 $\frac{17}{18} \div 4$

10 $\frac{12}{13} \div 3$

11 $\frac{2}{3} \div 6$

12 $\frac{5}{11} \div 20$

13 $\frac{3}{7} \div 11$

14 $\frac{1}{3} \div 9$

15 $\frac{10}{11} \div 5$

16 $\frac{10}{13} \div 3$

17 $\frac{4}{5} \div 4$

18 $\frac{12}{13} \div 5$

19 $\frac{2}{11} \div 4$

20 $\frac{3}{4} \div 7$

21 Mrs. Spinosa brought $\frac{15}{19}$ pounds of chocolate for her 4th grade class to enjoy. If all 15 students want an equal portion of chocolate, how much will each student receive?

_____

22 Mr. Lewis bought $\frac{10}{13}$ liters of apple cider to divide equally among his three children. How much apple cider will each child receive?

_____

Dividing Whole Numbers by Fractions

To divide a whole number by a fraction, you have to remember that a reciprocal is a fraction turned upside-down. For example, $\frac{2}{5}$ is the reciprocal of $\frac{5}{2}$, and $\frac{5}{2}$ is the reciprocal of $\frac{2}{5}$. To divide a whole number by a fraction, multiply the whole number by the reciprocal of the fraction.

Example: Divide: $4 \div \frac{3}{4}$

Step 1: Find the reciprocal of the fraction. The reciprocal of $\frac{3}{4}$ is $\frac{4}{3}$

Step 2: Multiply the whole number by the fraction's reciprocal. $4 \times \frac{4}{3} = \frac{16}{3}$

Remember...

A whole number can always be expressed as a fraction, with 1 as the denominator. So $2 = \frac{2}{1}$. When you divide a fraction by a whole number, you are *really* multiplying the fraction by the whole number's reciprocal. So $\frac{5}{8} \div 2 = \frac{5}{8} \div \frac{2}{1} = \frac{5}{8} \times \frac{1}{2} = \frac{5}{16}$.

Exercises DIVIDE

1. $5 \div \frac{1}{4}$
2. $3 \div \frac{4}{5}$
3. $7 \div \frac{1}{7}$
4. $9 \div \frac{4}{7}$
5. $2 \div \frac{1}{2}$

6. $4 \div \frac{2}{7}$
7. $15 \div \frac{5}{7}$
8. $4 \div \frac{2}{9}$
9. $17 \div \frac{2}{3}$
10. $5 \div \frac{3}{5}$

11. $6 \div \frac{2}{3}$
12. $9 \div \frac{3}{2}$
13. $5 \div \frac{1}{11}$
14. $14 \div \frac{7}{2}$
15. $3 \div \frac{1}{9}$

16. $3 \div \frac{7}{2}$
17. $5 \div \frac{3}{11}$
18. $11 \div \frac{22}{3}$
19. $18 \div \frac{3}{13}$
20. $7 \div \frac{1}{21}$

21. $16 \div \frac{4}{17}$
22. $4 \div \frac{1}{19}$
23. $21 \div \frac{7}{3}$
24. $55 \div \frac{11}{10}$
25. $23 \div \frac{46}{51}$

6.3

Dividing Fractions by Fractions

To divide a fraction by another fraction, multiply the first fraction by the reciprocal of the second fraction.

Example: Divide: $\frac{2}{3} \div \frac{6}{7}$

Step 1: Find the reciprocal of the second fraction. The reciprocal of $\frac{6}{7}$ is $\frac{7}{6}$

Step 2: Multiply the first fraction by the reciprocal of the second fraction.
$\frac{2}{3} \times \frac{7}{6}$

Step 3: Multiply the numerators.
$2 \times 7 = 14$

Step 4: Multiply the denominators:
$3 \times 6 = 18$

Step 5: Write the product: $\frac{14}{18}$. The product of that multiplication is *also* the quotient of the original division problem.

Step 6: Reduce the fraction if possible.
$\frac{14}{18} = \frac{7}{9}$

Remember...

When you divide fractions, you will *multiply* by the reciprocal!

Exercises   DIVIDE

1. $\frac{5}{7} \div \frac{3}{4}$ 2. $\frac{2}{3} \div \frac{2}{7}$ 3. $\frac{1}{9} \div \frac{3}{7}$ 4. $\frac{3}{4} \div \frac{1}{9}$ 5. $\frac{3}{13} \div \frac{2}{9}$

6. $\frac{1}{9} \div \frac{1}{3}$ 7. $\frac{2}{13} \div \frac{1}{5}$ 8. $\frac{3}{13} \div \frac{2}{13}$ 9. $\frac{4}{3} \div \frac{1}{4}$ 10. $\frac{15}{4} \div \frac{4}{3}$

11. $\frac{6}{7} \div \frac{1}{7}$ 12. $\frac{3}{17} \div \frac{4}{17}$ 13. $\frac{1}{11} \div \frac{22}{3}$ 14. $\frac{3}{7} \div \frac{1}{21}$ 15. $\frac{5}{14} \div \frac{1}{7}$

Dividing Mixed Numbers

To divide mixed numbers, change each mixed number into an improper fraction. If only one number in your division problem is a mixed number, change *it* to an improper fraction.

If *both* numbers in your division problem are mixed numbers, change *both* to improper fractions.

Example: Divide: $5\frac{1}{2} \div 2\frac{2}{3}$

Step 1: Change the first mixed number to an improper fraction. $5\frac{1}{2} = \frac{11}{2}$

Step 2: Change the second mixed number to an improper fraction. $2\frac{2}{3} = \frac{8}{3}$

Step 3: Restate the problem. $5\frac{1}{2} \div 2\frac{2}{3}$ is the same as $\frac{11}{2} \div \frac{8}{3}$

Step 4: Find the reciprocal of the second fraction. The reciprocal of $\frac{8}{3}$ is $\frac{3}{8}$

Step 5: Multiply the first fraction by the reciprocal of the second fraction. $\frac{11}{2} \times \frac{3}{8}$

Step 6: Multiply the numerators: $11 \times 3 = 33$

Step 7: Multiply the denominators: $2 \times 8 = 16$

Step 8: Write the product $\frac{33}{16}$. The product of that multiplication is *also* the quotient of the original division problem.

Step 9: Change the quotient to a mixed number.
$\frac{33}{16} = 2\frac{1}{16}$
$5\frac{1}{2} \div 2\frac{2}{3} = 2\frac{1}{16}$

Exercises DIVIDE

1. $1\frac{1}{2} \div 2\frac{1}{2}$

2. $3\frac{3}{5} \div 1\frac{1}{8}$

3. $7\frac{1}{7} \div 3\frac{1}{3}$

4. $3\frac{4}{7} \div 2\frac{2}{5}$

5. $6\frac{4}{5} \div 3\frac{2}{5}$

6. $5\frac{1}{2} \div 3\frac{3}{4}$

7. $4\frac{2}{9} \div 2\frac{4}{9}$

8. $9\frac{2}{7} \div 2\frac{1}{2}$

9. Frankie was making batches of cookies to bring to the school activities meeting. The recipe called for $1\frac{3}{4}$ cups of flour per batch. He had $5\frac{1}{4}$ cups of flour left in a bag. How many batches of cookies can Frankie bake?

_____

10. Jonas was making balloon decorations for the school dance. Each balloon needs $3\frac{2}{3}$ feet of ribbon to tie it down to the refreshment table. He has $51\frac{1}{3}$ feet of ribbon. How many balloons can he secure to the table?

_____

7.1

Ratios

A **ratio** compares two numbers by using division.

Example:

Six people want to share one pizza. Of course, each person wants the same size slice. To find out what part of the pizza each person gets, set up a ratio.

Divide: 1 pizza ÷ 6 people

Step 1: Express the problem as a fraction. $\dfrac{1\ \text{pizza}}{6\ \text{people}}$

Step 2: Remove the words. $\dfrac{1}{6}$

By using a ratio, you found that if you cut one pizza into six equal parts, each person gets $\dfrac{1}{6}$ of the pizza.

Exercises   SOLVE

1 A group of 7 friends has 15 dollars to share. What is each person's share?

_____

2 Gail rode her bicycle 325 miles in 5 days. How many miles did she ride each day?

_____

3 A diesel engine uses 100 quarts of oil for cooling. If the engine has 6 cylinders, how many quarts are there per cylinder?

_____

4 Jack used 6 pounds of butter in a recipe for 30 loaves of bread. How much butter did he use for each loaf of bread?

_____

5 It took 75 tons of gravel to cover 3 miles of road. How much gravel was used for each mile?

_____

6 At a restaurant, 6 people want to share 3 pizzas. If there are 8 slices in every pizza, how many slices does each person get?

_____

7 If a house has 2,000 square feet of wall surface to be painted and Marcia has already painted 1,600 square feet, what portion of the wall still needs to be painted?

_____

8 Tom put 8 gallons of gasoline into a 23-gallon tank. How much of the tank did he fill?

_____

Proportions and Cross-Multiplying

A **proportion** is a problem that contains two ratios that are equal. In a proportion problem, one of the numerators or one of the denominators is not known. The method for finding the missing numerator or denominator is called **cross-multiplying**.

Example:

A recipe calls for 3 tablespoons of nuts in order to make nutty pancakes for 5 people. How many tablespoons of nuts do you need to make nutty pancakes for 15 people?

Step 1: Express a proportion problem that uses two ratios.

$$\frac{3 \text{ tablespoons}}{5 \text{ people}} = \frac{(\text{how many tablespoons?})}{15 \text{ people}}$$

Step 2: Remove the words. $\frac{3}{5} = \frac{?}{15}$

Let's use t (for tablespoons) for the number we do not know. $\frac{3}{5} = \frac{t}{15}$

Step 3: To cross-multiply, you must set up an **equation**. An equation is a mathematical statement that two things are equal.

Step 4: On one side of the equal sign, write the first numerator × the second denominator.
$3 \times 15 =$

Step 5: On the other side of the equals sign, write the multiplication of the first denominator × the second numerator. $3 \times 15 = 5 \times t$

Step 6: Multiply the side that does *not* have the unknown number. $45 = 5 \times t$

Step 7: Look at the side that has both a known number and the unknown number. Divide *both* sides of the equation by the known number. (In this equation, that number is 5). You need 9 tablespoons of nuts to make nutty pancakes for 15 people.

Remember...

When you divide both sides of an equation by the *same* number, the expressions on both sides remain equal.

Exercises   SOLVE FOR x

① $\frac{4}{7} = \frac{x}{28}$

② $\frac{3}{5} = \frac{12}{x}$

③ $\frac{12}{x} = \frac{36}{51}$

④ $\frac{2}{3} = \frac{x}{21}$

⑤ $\frac{x}{14} = \frac{2}{7}$

⑥ $\frac{10}{55} = \frac{x}{11}$

⑦ $\frac{33}{44} = \frac{3}{x}$

⑧ $\frac{3}{51} = \frac{1}{x}$

Name _____

9 $\dfrac{39}{63} = \dfrac{x}{126}$ **10** $\dfrac{49}{14} = \dfrac{7}{x}$ **11** $\dfrac{5}{11} = \dfrac{x}{121}$ **12** $\dfrac{4}{13} = \dfrac{x}{52}$

13 $\dfrac{7}{8} = \dfrac{91}{x}$ **14** $\dfrac{10}{31} = \dfrac{110}{x}$ **15** $\dfrac{19}{57} = \dfrac{4}{x}$ **16** $\dfrac{13}{117} = \dfrac{x}{27}$

17 $\dfrac{4}{7} = \dfrac{x}{35}$ **18** $\dfrac{22}{x} = \dfrac{5}{110}$ **19** $\dfrac{x}{130} = \dfrac{7}{91}$ **20** $\dfrac{18}{6} = \dfrac{81}{x}$

21 $\dfrac{10}{121} = \dfrac{220}{x}$ **22** $\dfrac{7}{3} = \dfrac{x}{27}$ **23** $\dfrac{23}{4} = \dfrac{92}{x}$ **24** $\dfrac{x}{17} = \dfrac{48}{68}$

25 $\dfrac{12}{x} = \dfrac{2}{7}$ **26** $\dfrac{7}{x} = \dfrac{70}{120}$ **27** $\dfrac{3}{4} = \dfrac{123}{x}$ **28** $\dfrac{x}{55} = \dfrac{28}{220}$

Rates

Sometimes, you will be asked to solve a problem about rates. A rate is a fixed ratio between two things. For example: Maria drives at a rate of 65 miles per hour. How many hours does it take her to drive 195 miles? Notice that this is really a proportion problem.

Example:

Step 1: Express the proportion problem using two ratios. In this problem, let's use h for the unknown number of hours. $\frac{1}{65} = \frac{h}{195}$

Step 2: Use the proportion problem to set up an equation. Then cross-multiply. $195 = 65 \times h$

Step 3: Find the side of the equation with the unknown number. Then look at the known number on that side. (In this equation, it is 65.) Divide *both* sides of the equation by that known number. $195 \div 65 = h$

It will take Maria 3 hours to drive 195 miles!

Exercises   SOLVE

1 Bob eats 6 apples in 2 days. How many days will it take for him to eat a basket of apples containing 51 apples?

_____

2 Fay travels 56 kilometers in 8 hours. How many kilometers will she travel in a day?

_____

3 Bob can paint the lines in the middle of the road at a rate of 18 miles in a 9-hour work day. How many miles can he paint on Saturday when he works 5 hours?

_____

4 In the first 3 hours of a concert, 2,100 people passed through the gates. How long will it take to fill a concert hall that has 2,800 seats?

_____

5 5 horses can plow 20 acres of land in an hour. How many acres can 21 horses plow in an hour?

_____

6 How many minutes will it take 5 people to stack 250 chairs if each person can stack 20 chairs a minute?

_____

7 George can polish 240 square feet of floor in 2 hours. How many square feet can he polish in 7 hours?

_____

8 It took 35 minutes for the first 45 people to pass through customs at the airport. If it takes the same amount of time for each person, how long will it take for the whole plane of 135 people to pass through customs?

_____

Problem-Solving with Proportions

There are many kinds of proportion problems that you may run across in real life. Just remember the basic steps:

Step 1: Express your proportion problem using two ratios.

Step 2: Use your proportion problem to set up an equation with cross-multiplication.

Step 3: To find the unknown number, divide both sides of the equation by the same number.

Exercises   SOLVE FOR x

1 If a car can travel 105 miles on 7 gallons of gas, how far can it travel on 9 gallons of gas?

_____

2 A farmer uses 3 tons of fertilizer on 14 acres of land. How many acres can he fertilize with 45 tons?

_____

3 It takes Kenny 25 minutes to inflate the tires of 55 bicycles, how long will it take him to inflate the tires of 121 bicycles?

_____

4 How many pizzas do you need for a party of 135 people if at the last party, 90 people ate 52 pizzas? (Assume the same rate of consumption.)

_____

5 Jim spent $55 at the last yard sale when he bought 14 items. If he sees 24 items that he liked at the yard sale across the street, how much money should he expect to spend? (Assume he spends the same amount per item.)

_____

6 Kim wants to expand her lawn mowing business. She presently mows 58 lawns with 6 workers. How many workers will she need if she plans to mow a total of 87 lawns?

_____

7 At the apple orchard, each row of 7 apple trees yields 78 bushels of apples. If there are 112 trees in the orchard, how many bushels of apples should you expect to be harvested?

_____

8 Each troop of 32 girl scouts eats 11 pounds of cereal a week. If there are 45 troops at the scout camp, how many pounds of cereal should be purchased?

_____

Lessons 4–7

Change to mixed numbers.

1 $\frac{15}{7}$

2 $\frac{23}{5}$

3 $\frac{85}{17}$

4 $\frac{311}{34}$

_____   _____   _____   _____

Change to improper fractions.

5 $8\frac{6}{7}$

6 $14\frac{4}{9}$

7 $3\frac{17}{23}$

8 $4\frac{7}{31}$

_____   _____   _____   _____

Add or subtract and reduce to simplest form.

9 $\frac{3}{4} + \frac{1}{4}$

10 $\frac{10}{43} - \frac{5}{43}$

11 $\frac{5}{7} + \frac{3}{7}$

12 $\frac{23}{59} + \frac{24}{59}$

_____   _____   _____   _____

13 $\frac{45}{47} - \frac{34}{47}$

14 $\frac{12}{35} + \frac{18}{35}$

15 $\frac{65}{94} - \frac{18}{94}$

16 $\frac{33}{73} + \frac{23}{73}$

_____   _____   _____   _____

17 $3\frac{3}{7} - 2\frac{2}{7}$

18 $\frac{23}{33} + \frac{17}{21}$

19 $\frac{3}{7} + \frac{4}{5}$

20 $\frac{14}{25} - \frac{12}{29}$

_____   _____   _____   _____

21 $\frac{4}{9} + \frac{1}{11}$

22 $\frac{17}{19} - \frac{2}{3}$

23 $\frac{1}{2} - \frac{19}{39}$

24 $\frac{8}{17} + \frac{9}{19}$

_____   _____   _____   _____

Lessons 4–7

25 $4\frac{14}{23} - 2\frac{17}{23}$ _____

26 $10\frac{32}{63} + 15\frac{34}{63}$ _____

27 $12\frac{23}{29} + 11\frac{17}{29}$ _____

28 $11\frac{4}{7} + 3\frac{3}{4}$ _____

Multiply.

29 $\frac{1}{2} \times 45$ _____

30 $\frac{3}{4} \times 44$ _____

31 $\frac{9}{4} \times 60$ _____

32 $12 \times \frac{12}{23}$ _____

33 $\frac{2}{3} \times 4\frac{4}{9}$ _____

34 $6 \times \frac{3}{7}$ _____

35 $\frac{26}{29} \times 13$ _____

36 $\frac{34}{47} \times 17$ _____

Divide.

37 $\frac{2}{3} \div 36$ _____

38 $\frac{4}{9} \div 3$ _____

39 $\frac{45}{63} \div 15$ _____

40 $9 \div \frac{6}{7}$ _____

41 $25 \div \frac{15}{24}$ _____

42 $45 \div \frac{5}{9}$ _____

43 $\frac{3}{4} \div \frac{14}{25}$ _____

44 $\frac{4}{7} \div \frac{7}{4}$ _____

45 $\frac{13}{57} \div \frac{26}{19}$ _____

46 $2\frac{2}{3} \div 8\frac{3}{4}$ _____

47 $12\frac{3}{4} \div 4\frac{3}{4}$ _____

48 $15\frac{3}{5} \div 2\frac{1}{5}$ _____

Unit Test

Lessons 4–7

Create a ratio and reduce to simplest form.

49 8 people want to share a large pizza. Use a ratio to express how much of the pizza each person will receive if the pizza is divided equally. _____

50 In the school parking lot, there are 5 red cars and 25 black cars. Express this as a ratio. _____

Determine if the following proportions are equal. (Write Yes or No.)

51 $\frac{4}{5} = \frac{25}{20}$ _____

52 $\frac{7}{12} = \frac{28}{36}$ _____

53 $\frac{2}{19} = \frac{38}{4}$ _____

54 $\frac{3}{4} = \frac{18}{24}$ _____

55 Wally rides his bicycle at an average speed of 13 miles per hour. How many miles will he travel in $4\frac{1}{2}$ hours? _____

56 Jasmine can make 49 cupcakes in a batch. How many batches of cupcakes does she need to make 323 cupcakes? _____

57 Phillip drinks $\frac{2}{3}$ pint of water for each mile he runs. How many pints of water will he drink if he runs $4\frac{1}{2}$ miles? _____

58 Perry texts his friends 2,337 times in 21 days. Will he go over his limit of 3,000 texts in the 30-day billing period? _____

59 Glenn's car burns 2 quarts of oil every 1,750 miles. How many quarts of oil should he buy if he plans to take a trip of 3,275 miles? _____

Name _____

Decimal Place Value and Rounding

Sometimes you will be asked to round a number with a decimal to the nearest whole number. You need to look at the number on the right side of the decimal point. If that number is less than five, keep the whole number as it is. If that number is 5 or greater, add 1 to the whole number.

Tens	Ones		Tenths	Hundredths	Thousandths
6	3	.	5	1	2

Example: Round 63.512 to a whole number.

Step 1: Look only at the number to the immediate right of the decimal point. 5

Step 2: Ask yourself: Is that number 5 or greater? Yes.

Step 3: Add 1 to the whole number. $63 + 1 = 64$

In other exercises, you might need to round a decimal to the nearest tenth, the nearest hundredth, or the nearest thousandth. Always look at the number to the *right* of the place you are rounding to. For example, if you are rounding to tenths, look at the hundredths place. If the number you look at is less than 5, keep the original number, *but only to the place you need*. If that number is 5 or greater, add 1 to *that* place.

Example: Round 5.18499 to the nearest hundredths.

Step 1: Look at the place to the right of the hundredths place. (It will be the number in the thousandths place.)

Step 2: Ask yourself: Is that number 5 or greater? No.

Step 3: Keep the original decimal *up to the place you need.* 5.18

Exercises   ROUND

Round to the nearest whole number.

1. 68.1   2. 17.7   3. 22.2   4. 47.5   5. 76.4

_____ _____ _____ _____ _____

Round to the nearest tenth.

6. 18.47   7. 21.23   8. 44.44   9. 11.14   10. 59.49

_____ _____ _____ _____ _____

Round to the nearest hundredth.

11. 429.345   12. 39.746   13. 313.313   14. 528.456   15. 832.832

_____ _____ _____ _____ _____

Round to the nearest thousandth.

16. 32.3456   17. 1.4141   18. 12.1728   19. 592.4219   20. 837.8198

_____ _____ _____ _____ _____

Changing Fractions to Decimals

A decimal is really a fraction expressed in another way. So $\frac{3}{10} = 0.3$, and $3\frac{17}{100} = 3.17$.

Decimals are expressed in tenths, hundredths, thousandths, and so on. However, you can convert a fraction into a decimal. Just divide the fraction's numerator by its denominator.

Example: What decimal equals $\frac{1}{4}$?

Step 1: $\frac{1}{4} = 1 \div 4$ Set this up as a regular division problem: $4\overline{)1}$. However, 4 does not go into 1. You need to add a decimal point to the 1 and as many placeholder zeros as necessary for you to divide. You must also use a decimal point in the quotient. Be sure to line it up with the decimal point in the dividend.

Step 2: Add a decimal point and one placeholder zero. Then add a decimal point to the quotient.

$$4\overline{)1.0}$$

Step 3: Begin dividing.

$$\begin{array}{r} .2 \\ 4\overline{)1.0} \\ \underline{8} \\ 2 \end{array}$$

Step 4: If you have a remainder, add another placeholder zero.

$$\begin{array}{r} .25 \\ 4\overline{)1.0} \\ \underline{8} \\ 20 \\ \underline{20} \\ 0 \end{array}$$

Step 5: Keep adding placeholder zeros until you have no remainder. If you have already added four placeholder zeros, think about rounding your decimal to the nearest thousandths place.

Remember...

A rounded decimal will not *exactly* equal the fraction you started with.

Exercises **CHANGE FRACTIONS TO DECIMALS**

Round to the nearest ten thousandth, if necessary.

1 $\frac{1}{4}$ 2 $\frac{7}{8}$ 3 $\frac{1}{9}$ 4 $\frac{5}{7}$ 5 $\frac{5}{11}$

_____   _____   _____   _____   _____

6 $\frac{7}{19}$ 7 $\frac{15}{78}$ 8 $\frac{43}{44}$ 9 $\frac{3}{23}$ 10 $\frac{8}{15}$

_____   _____   _____   _____   _____

Name _____

Changing Decimals to Fractions

Changing decimals to fractions is easier than changing fractions to decimals. Look at the place value farthest to the right, and use that as your denominator. Use the actual decimal as your numerator.

Example: Change .36 to a fraction.

Step 1: Look at the place value. Use it as your denominator. The place value farthest to the right in .36 is the hundredths place. So the denominator will be 100.

Step 2: Use the decimal as the numerator. $\frac{36}{100}$

Step 3: Simplify the fraction if you can. Divide the numerator and the denominator by the same number. $\frac{36 \div 4}{100 \div 4} = \frac{9}{25}$

Exercises — CHANGE DECIMALS TO FRACTIONS

1 .45 _____

2 .470 _____

3 1.4 _____

4 .68 _____

5 .22 _____

6 .25 _____

7 3.75 _____

8 .8125 _____

9 1.875 _____

10 .11 _____

11 .8 _____

12 .125 _____

13 .65 _____

14 .53 _____

15 .44 _____

16 A recipe calls for 1.375 cups of flour to be mixed together with .125 cups of corn starch. If Stefano has only a $\frac{1}{8}$ measuring cup to measure the flour and corn starch, how many measuring cups full of flour and how many measuring cups of corn starch will he need to fill to complete the recipe?

_____ measuring cups of flour

_____ measuring cups of corn starch

17 Alphonse uses a pedometer to record how far he walks during his morning workout. After walking a while, he rests and notices that the pedometer shows he has walked .9 miles. If he walks $1\frac{4}{5}$ miles every day as part of his workout, how much farther does Alphonse need to walk to finish his workout? _____

Name _____

Comparing and Ordering Decimals

When you compare whole numbers, you look at place value. To compare decimals, you will look at place value. Line up your decimals so that the decimal points are in a column. Then begin by looking at the column to the immediate *right* of the decimal point, the tenths place. As you arrange your numbers, work toward the *right*.

Example: Place these decimals in order from least to greatest.
.31   .186   0.7   .09   .34   .091

Step 1: Line up the decimal points.
.31
.186
0.7
.09
.34
.091

Step 2: Find the greatest number in the tenths place. 0.7

Step 3: Find the next greatest number in the tenths place. .31 and .34

Step 4: If two decimals have the same number in the tenths place, you must look at the next place value, the hundredths place. With .31 and .34, 4 is greater than 1.

Step 5: Continue to put all decimals in the correct order.
0.7
.34
.31
.186

What do you do with .09 and .091?

Add a zero to .09 as a placeholder for the thousandths place. That gives you .090. Now, when you look at the thousandths place, you can see that .091 is slightly greater!

Remember...

When comparing numbers with decimals, always look at the whole numbers first. If two whole numbers are the same, *then* compare *to the right* from the decimal point.

Exercises   COMPARE AND ORDER

Put the numbers in order from least to greatest.

1   .33   .333   .3333

2   .39   1.39   .388   .393

3   4.44   4.441   .44   4.439

4   7.78   7.7778   7.778   7.7777

5   4.45   44.5   .445   445

6   22.2323   22.2332   22.3   22.23222

7   1.765   1.7655   1.766   1.76559

8   .09   1.09   .08888   .090001

9   9.98989   9.998989   9.999888   9.9999888

Name _____

Adding Decimals

Adding decimals is *just like* adding whole numbers, except that you must be careful to line up the decimals correctly. Once you do that, you can add as if the decimal is not there.

Example: Add 85.38 + 6.99

Step 1: Line up the numbers. Make sure that the decimal points line up in a column.

```
  85.38
+  6.99
```

Step 2: Place a decimal point in the answer line under the other decimal points.

```
  85.38
+  6.99
      .
```

Step 3: Add:

```
  85.38
+  6.99
  92.37
```

What if a number has no decimal point? For example: Add 17 + 34.972
Just put a decimal point at the end of the whole number and write placeholder zeros.

```
  17.000
+ 34.972
  51.972
```

Exercises   ADD

1
```
  1.345
+ 2.34
```

2
```
  7.772
+ 3.333
```

3
```
  1.23
+ .123
```

4
```
   12.35
+ 125.43
```

5
```
   4.4224
+ 44.2442
```

6
```
  53.111
+  .3341
```

7
```
  .251
+ 2.51
```

8
```
  10.101
+   .990
```

9
```
  11.1
+ 11.111
```

10
```
  113.31
+  31.113
```

11
```
  345
+ .345
```

12
```
  239.54
+  23.454
```

13
```
  525.525
+  52.5525
```

14
```
  101.55
+   .101
```

15 Hailey is on the school track team. Her event is the triple jump. In her last meet the "hop" portion of her jump was 12.256 feet, the "skip" 11.114 feet, and the "jump" portion was 13.4455 feet. How far did she jump in total?

_____

16 During a flight to the International Space Station, the space shuttle pilot had to conduct a mid-course correction by firing the shuttle's rockets three times lasting 12.354 seconds, 11.4538 seconds, and 9.7392 seconds. What is the total time the rockets were fired?

_____

Subtracting Decimals

Subtracting decimals is *just like* subtracting whole numbers. However, you must correctly line up the decimals. Write placeholder zeros if you need to.

Example: Subtract 173.29 − 97.6

Step 1: Line up the numbers. Make sure that the decimal points line up. Write placeholder zeros if you need to. Place a decimal point in the answer line under the other decimal points.

```
  173.29
−  97.60
       .
```

Step 2: Subtract.

```
  173.29
−  97.60
   75.69
```

See if you can figure out how to provide an answer for this exercise. Perform this subtraction: 62 − 11.73 If you added a decimal point and placeholder zeros to the whole number, you were correct!

```
  62.00
− 11.73
  50.27
```

Remember...

The value of a number does not change if you add a decimal point and placeholder zeros. Add as many placeholder zeros as you need in order to solve the problem.

Exercises   SUBTRACT

1.
```
  23.01
− 22.99
```

2.
```
  113.525
−  45.67
```

3.
```
  32.11
− 11.99
```

4.
```
  10.25
−   .75
```

5.
```
  45.54
− 33.522
```

6.
```
  14.6
− 14.444
```

7.
```
  32.004
− 11.01
```

8.
```
  222.3
−  41.22
```

9.
```
  6.19
− 4.334
```

10.
```
  8.565
−  .006
```

11.
```
  345.34
−  53.678
```

12.
```
  53.7
−  4.88
```

13.
```
  2.398
− 1.998
```

14.
```
  717
−  33.71
```

15.
```
  3
− 1.52
```

16.
```
  32.3
− 21.28
```

Name _____

Adding and Subtracting Money

You may not realize it, but you work with a great many decimals in your life.

Look at this problem: $98.42 + $11.79

American money is written in decimals. A dollar is divided into 100 hundredths, each of which is called "a cent." If something costs 11 dollars and 79 cents, it really costs 11 dollars + 79 hundredths of a dollar.

Adding and subtracting money is done *exactly* the same way as adding and subtracting decimals.

Example: Add $98.42 + $11.79

Step 1: Line up the decimals.

$$\begin{array}{r} \$\ 98.42 \\ +\ \$\ 11.79 \\ \hline \end{array}$$

Step 2: Add, just as you would any other decimals.

$$\begin{array}{r} \$\ 98.42 \\ +\ \$\ 11.79 \\ \hline \$110.21 \end{array}$$

Remember...

You can add placeholder zeros to money, too. Doing this does not change its value! For example, $35 = $35.**00**

Exercises   ADD OR SUBTRACT

1
$$\begin{array}{r} \$5 \\ +\ \$5.67 \\ \hline \end{array}$$

2
$$\begin{array}{r} \$3.45 \\ +\ \$133.56 \\ \hline \end{array}$$

3
$$\begin{array}{r} \$10.87 \\ +\ \$21.65 \\ \hline \end{array}$$

4
$$\begin{array}{r} \$11 \\ -\ \$4.55 \\ \hline \end{array}$$

5
$$\begin{array}{r} \$6.77 \\ -\ \$3.88 \\ \hline \end{array}$$

6
$$\begin{array}{r} \$12.30 \\ -\ \$5.45 \\ \hline \end{array}$$

7
$$\begin{array}{r} \$20.50 \\ -\ \$15.39 \\ \hline \end{array}$$

8
$$\begin{array}{r} \$62.32 \\ -\ \$7.54 \\ \hline \end{array}$$

9
$$\begin{array}{r} \$22.22 \\ +\ \$11.33 \\ \hline \end{array}$$

10
$$\begin{array}{r} \$65 \\ +\ \$33 \\ \hline \end{array}$$

11
$$\begin{array}{r} \$5.12 \\ +\ \$3.50 \\ \hline \end{array}$$

12
$$\begin{array}{r} \$71.42 \\ +\ \$36.54 \\ \hline \end{array}$$

13
$$\begin{array}{r} \$1000 \\ -\ \$312.80 \\ \hline \end{array}$$

14
$$\begin{array}{r} \$21.10 \\ -\ \$11.33 \\ \hline \end{array}$$

15
$$\begin{array}{r} \$2.25 \\ -\ \$0.30 \\ \hline \end{array}$$

16
$$\begin{array}{r} \$45.53 \\ -\ \$32.55 \\ \hline \end{array}$$

17
$$\begin{array}{r} \$12.30 \\ -\ \$11.98 \\ \hline \end{array}$$

18
$$\begin{array}{r} \$56 \\ -\ \$37.98 \\ \hline \end{array}$$

19
$$\begin{array}{r} \$33 \\ -\ \$12 \\ \hline \end{array}$$

20
$$\begin{array}{r} \$41.65 \\ -\ \$38.78 \\ \hline \end{array}$$

Estimating Decimal Sums and Differences

You can use rounding to estimate sums and differences of decimal numbers. However, you have to decide what rounding place to use. Sometimes, a problem will tell you. If it does not, round to the nearest whole number.

When estimating money, ask yourself: Is the cents part of each number closest to 0 dollars, to a $\frac{1}{2}$ dollar, or to a dollar?

Example: Estimate 5.87 + 7.061

Step 1: Round 5.87 to the nearest whole number. 6

Step 2: Round 7.061 to the nearest whole number. 7

Step 3: Add: 6 + 7 = 13

The sum of 5.87 + 7.061 is *about* 13.

Example: 17.365 – 14.229 to the nearest tenth

Step 1: Round 17.365 to the nearest tenth. 17.4

Step 2: Round 14.229 to the nearest tenth. 14.2

Step 3: Subtract: 17.4 – 14.2 = 3.2

Example: Estimate $7.37 + $9.89

Step 1: Ask yourself: Is $7.37 closer to $7.00, $7.50, or $8.00? $7.50

Step 2: Ask yourself: Is $9.89 closer to $9.00, $9.50, or $10.00? $10.00

Step 3: Add: $7.50 + $10.00 = $17.50

Since you rounded *both* dollar amounts up, you know that your estimated total is *higher* than the actual total.

Exercises   ESTIMATE

1   44.55
     + 5.67

2   34.57
     + 24.57

3   75.55
     − 9.45

4   4.55
     + 4.9

5   9.6
     − 3.5

6 $7.82
     + $11.54

7   12.78
     − 11.6

8 $34.89
     − $24.7

9   54.55
     − 7.65

10 $15.4
      − $9.6

11   12.78
      + 77.34

12   49.78
      − 41.22

Multiplying Decimals

Multiplying decimals and whole numbers is *exactly like* multiplying whole numbers—except for one important thing. You have to count the *total* decimal places in the numbers you multiply. When you multiply decimals, you do *not* have to line up the decimal points.

Example: Multiply. 22.6 × 3.21
Then multiply .226 × .321

Step 1: Set up your multiplication exercise as you would any other multiplication exercise. Do *not* line up the decimal points.

$$22.6 \qquad\qquad .226$$
$$\times\ 3.21 \qquad\qquad \times\ .321$$

Step 2: Multiply. At this time, pay no attention to the decimal points.

```
   22.6              .226
 × 3.21            × .321
   226               226
  4520              4520
 67800             67800
 72546             72546
```

Step 3: Count the *total* number of decimal places in the **factors**. Factors are the numbers you multiplied. 22.6 has 1 decimal place. 3.21 has 2 decimal places. 1 + 2 = 3

Step 4: Starting at the right of the product and moving *left*, count off the same number of places. Then place your decimal point. The product of
22.6 × 3.21 = 72.546
└— three decimal places

Step 5: But what about .226 × .321? There are six decimal places in those factors, but only five places in the product. The answer is: You have to add enough zeros to make the *total* number of places in the product equal the total number of decimal places in the numbers you multiplied. Add the needed zeros *after* the decimal point. So the product of
.226 × .321 = .072546
└— six decimal places

Remember...

A power of ten is the number of times you multiply by 10. Each column is 10 times the column to its right. For example:

1 × 10 = 10; 1 × 10 × 10 = 100;

1 × 10 × 10 × 10 = 1000

.1 × 10 = 1; .01 × 10 = .1; .001 × 10 = .01

Here is a trick: If you multiply a whole number or a decimal by a power of ten that is greater than 1, move the decimal point 1 place to the right for each power of 10. If you need more places, add placeholder zeros at the end of the whole number. If you multiply by a power of 10 that is less than 1, move the decimal point one place to the left for each decimal place in the power of 10.

Exercises MULTIPLY

1
```
   415
 × 23.1
```

2
```
     7
 × 7.77
```

3
```
 324.56
 ×    54
```

4
```
 10.01
 ×   11
```

5
```
   3232
 × 42.42
```

6 87.3
× 233

7 65.8
× 68

8 120
× 14.56

9 438
× 1.1

10 14.7
× 101

11 10.1
× 1.01

12 55.5
× 5.55

13 41.0
× 4.41

14 13.82
× 10.51

15 21.12
× 81.93

16 2.7
× 3.1

17 17.89
× 41.1

18 1.414
× 2.71

19 73.75
× 7.5

20 20.01
× 30.02

21 19.9
× 100

22 2.4
× 10

23 .001
× 112.34

24 1.56
× .01

25 71.782
× 1000

26 76.76
× 1000

27 10
× 1.32

28 63.45
× 1000

29 13.45
× .0001

30 1111.111
× .01

Name _____

Multiplying Money

Since American money is expressed as a decimal, you multiply money exactly as you would multiply decimals. However, there are two important things to remember about multiplying money.

First, you *cannot* multiply money times money. You can only multiply money by a number. However, that number *can* be a decimal.

Second, the product will *always* be money. Therefore, you *always* have to round the product to the nearest hundredth.

Example: Multiply $1.35 × 2.75

Step 1: Set up your multiplication.

$$\begin{array}{r} \$1.35 \\ \times\ 2.75 \end{array}$$

Step 2: Multiply.

$$\begin{array}{r} \$1.35 \\ \times\ 2.75 \\ \hline 675 \\ 9450 \\ 27000 \\ \hline 37125 \end{array}$$

Step 3: Count the decimal places in your two numbers and add the decimal point to the product. 2 decimal places in $1.35 + 2 decimal places in 2.75 = 4 decimal places. So the product is 3.7125.

Step 4: Round the product to the nearest hundredth and add the dollar sign. $3.71

Exercises MULTIPLY

1 $10.45 × 2.50

2 $101.91 × 1.1

3 $5.76 × 3.75

4 $78.90 × 9.92

5 $7.29 × 5.5

6 $89.21 × 3

7 $67.50 × 6.75

8 $10.00 × 2.3

9 $5.50 × 11

10 $4.75 × 9.5

11 $85.30 × 5

12 $33.00 × 2.2

13 Petra needs to buy gasoline for her car. Gasoline costs $3.66 for a gallon, and she needs 6.75 gallons to fill her tank. How much money will Petra need to spend, in order to fill her tank?

_____

14 Jerry is going to start a collection of marbles with the $5 he received for his weekly allowance. He wants at least 120 marbles to begin his collection. If each individual marble costs 4 cents, will he have enough money to buy 120?

_____

Estimating Decimal Products

To estimate decimal products, round each
number to its highest place value.

Examples: Estimate 121.9 × .352

Step 1: Round the first number to its highest place
value: 121.9 rounds to 100

Step 2: Round the second number to its highest
place value: .352 rounds to .4

Step 3: Multiply the rounded amounts:
100 × .4 = 40 (Did you notice that you
could use the trick you learned in Lesson
10.1?)

So a fairly good estimate of 121.9 × .352 is 40.

Estimate $4.99 × 1.75

Step 1: Round the first number to its highest place.
$4.99 rounds to 5

Step 2: Round the second number to its highest
place value.
1.75 rounds to 2

Step 3: Multiply the rounded amounts.
$5 × 2 = $10

Did you notice that you rounded both numbers
upward? That means your estimate is *higher* than
the actual product.

Exercises   ESTIMATE

1 23.01 × 8.1

2 $6.75 × 4.73

3 101.51 × 4.5

4 32.25 × 21.1

5 $2.25 × 49.999

6 .230 × 4.657

7 10.501 × $5.43

8 45.45 × 21.21

9 57.35 × .499

10 .867 × $19.3

11 .75 × 25.43

12 1.95 × 36.36

13 23.986 × 11.111

14 22.989 × $13.89

15 1.8 × 1.982

16 27.63 × $3.54

17 10.1010 × 7.3

18 7.75 × 4.1

19 17.11 × 1.499

20 $19.45 × 1.73

Name _____

Dividing Decimals by Whole Numbers

Dividing a decimal by a whole number is *exactly like* dividing whole numbers except that you have to know where to put the decimal point in your quotient.

If *only* the dividend has a decimal point, put the decimal point in exactly the same column in the quotient.

Example: Divide $25.8 \div 3$

Step 1: Set up your division problem and put the decimal point in its proper place in the quotient.

$$3\overline{)25.8}$$

Step 2: Divide.

$$
\begin{array}{r}
8.6 \\
3\overline{)25.8} \\
\underline{24} \\
18 \\
\underline{18} \\
0
\end{array}
$$

Exercises   DIVIDE

1 $2\overline{)10.1}$

2 $4\overline{)22.45}$

3 $10\overline{)78.25}$

4 $11\overline{)22.22}$

5 $8\overline{)7.75}$

6 $5\overline{)14.5}$

7 $20\overline{)77.8}$

8 $30\overline{)45.45}$

9 $6\overline{)104.0}$

10 $2\overline{)55.875}$

11 $4\overline{)101.56}$

12 $7\overline{)929.6}$

13 $8\overline{)2225.25}$

14 $29\overline{)116.58}$

15 $8\overline{)13.75}$

16 $7\overline{)742.21}$

Dividing Whole Numbers by Decimals

Dividing a whole number by a decimal is also *exactly like* dividing whole numbers, except that you need to remember to multiply the divisor by the smallest power of 10 that will move the decimal point all the way to the right. Then multiply the dividend by that same power of 10.

Example: Divide 45 ÷ .24

Step 1: Multiply the divisor by the smallest power of 10 that will move the decimal point all the way to the right: .24 × 100 = 24

Step 2: Multiply the dividend by the same power of 10: 45 × 100 = 4500

Step 3: Set up your division and divide.

```
      187 R12
24)4500.0
    24
    210
    192
     180
     168
      12
```

Instead of leaving a remainder, you can put a decimal point at the end of the dividend and add as many placeholder zeros as you need. Then continue dividing, but don't forget to put the decimal point in the quotient, too!

```
       187.5
24)4500.0
    24
    210
    192
     180
     168
      120
      120
        0
```

Exercises DIVIDE

1. .44)33

2. .2)521

3. .45)12

4. .1)453

5. .25)44

6. .56)21

7. .65)422

8. .05)200

9. .22)655

10. .12)76

11. .4)7

12. .11)222

Name _____

Dividing Decimals by Decimals

If you know how to divide a whole number by a decimal, you also know how to divide a decimal by a decimal.

Multiply the divisor by the smallest power of 10 that will move the decimal point all the way to the right. Then multiply the dividend by that same power of 10.

Example: Divide $4.29 \div 3.3$

Step 1: Multiply the divisor by the smallest power of 10 that will move the decimal point all the way to the right: $3.3 \times 10 = 33$

Step 2: Multiply the dividend by the same power of 10: $4.29 \times 10 = 42.9$

Step 3: Set up your division problem. If there is a decimal point in the dividend, line up a

decimal point in the same place in the quotient.

Step 4: Divide.

$$
\begin{array}{r}
1.3 \\
33\overline{)42.9} \\
\underline{33} \\
99 \\
\underline{99} \\
0
\end{array}
$$

Exercises DIVIDE

1 $.44\overline{).22}$

2 $3.12\overline{).2}$

3 $.56\overline{).33}$

4 $.76\overline{).03}$

5 $.89\overline{).4}$

6 $.784\overline{).08}$

7 $45.45\overline{).09}$

8 $87.5\overline{).07}$

9 Olga bought 3.75 pounds of candy that she will place in small boxes and give to her classmates at summer school. If each box hold .35 pounds of candy, how many boxes will she be able to fill?

_____

10 Omar and his friends are getting ready to go for a hike. Omar buys 21.2 liters of water to fill 17 canteens. If each canteen holds 1.3 liters, will Omar be able to fill all 17 canteens?

_____

Dividing Money

You know that American money can be expressed as a decimal. You divide money *exactly the same way* you would divide any other kind of decimal. The only thing you need to remember is: If you're dividing with money, money *must* be in your dividend, and in your quotient. The divisor might be money, or it might not. Since your quotient is money, it should always be rounded to the nearest hundredth.

You might want to divide a restaurant check by the number of people dining to find out what each person owes.

Three people ate lunch and the total came to $37.77 including the tip. How much should each person pay?

Step 1: Set up your division exercise. If there is a decimal point in the dividend, line up a decimal point in the same place in the quotient.

$$3\overline{)37.77}$$

Step 2: Divide:

$$
\begin{array}{r}
12.59 \\
3\overline{)37.77} \\
\underline{3} \\
7 \\
\underline{6} \\
17 \\
\underline{15} \\
27 \\
\underline{27} \\
0
\end{array}
$$

Exercises   DIVIDE

1   $3\overline{)\$1.35}$

2   $4\overline{)\$10.00}$

3   $10.1\overline{)\$56.45}$

4   $.8\overline{)\$27.95}$

5   $1.07\overline{)\$97.28}$

6   $6.4\overline{)\$54.67}$

7   $2.3\overline{)\$181.47}$

8   $8.5\overline{)\$774.35}$

9   $65.9\overline{)\$210.88}$

10   $64.3\overline{)\$135.03}$

11   $2.2\overline{)\$211.86}$

12   $63.2\overline{)\$132.72}$

13   $.02\overline{)\$8.48}$

14   $2.5\overline{)\$21.25}$

15   $3.7\overline{)\$207.94}$

16   $2.2\overline{)\$44.22}$

17   $5.8\overline{)\$15.66}$

18   $9.7\overline{)\$26.19}$

19   $44.9\overline{)\$152.66}$

20   $10.5\overline{)\$85.05}$

Estimating Decimal Quotients

How do you estimate a quotient when the dividend, the divisor, or both contain decimals? The easy answer is to forget about the decimals! There are two ways to do that. The first way is just to drop the decimals, and then round.

The second way is to round first, *then* drop the decimals. Estimating this way will often make your estimate better.

> **Example:** Estimate 35.89 ÷ 6.1
>
> **Step 1:** Drop the decimals: 35 ÷ 6
>
> **Step 2:** Find compatible numbers: 35 cannot be divided by 6, but 36 can.
>
> **Step 3:** Divide: 36 ÷ 6 = 6
>
> So a fairly good estimate of 35.89 ÷ 6.1 is 6.

> **Example:** Estimate 49.83 ÷ 4.76
>
> **Step 1:** Round both numbers to the nearest whole number. 49.83 rounds to 50 and 4.76 rounds to 5.
>
> **Step 2:** Divide the rounded numbers: 50 ÷ 5 = 10
>
> Notice that if you had estimated 49.83 ÷ 4.76 using the first method, you would have dropped the decimals and started with 49 ÷ 4. Your estimated answer would have been 12. The actual quotient of 49.83 ÷ 4.76 is about 10.47. Which method of estimating was closer to the actual value?

Exercises   ESTIMATE

1 14.6 ÷ 1.2   2 24.4 ÷ 8   3 9.1 ÷ 9   4 39.9 ÷ 13

5 41.2 ÷ 25   6 132.1 ÷ 13   7 44.73 ÷ 9   8 6.72 ÷ 3.3

9 4.41 ÷ .91   10 25.2 ÷ 2.3   11 49.3 ÷ 4   12 32.11 ÷ 8.0

13 12.47 ÷ 5.0   14 33.33 ÷ 1.6   15 56.4 ÷ 11   16 23.53 ÷ 2.0

17 88.97 ÷ 4.5   18 48.94 ÷ 2.4   19 77 ÷ 5.3   20 73.2 ÷ 9.4

Understanding Percent

Notice that the word *percent* has the smaller word *cent* in it. You know cent from dealing with money. Every dollar can be divided into 100 hundredths. Therefore, it probably will not surprise you that *cent* means *hundredth*. *Per* means *by*. A **percent** is a particular kind of ratio that is used to compare numbers to hundredths.

The % sign is used to identify percents. However, a percent is really a decimal that goes to the hundredths place. A percent can also be expressed as a fraction, with 100 as the denominator.

Examples: $1\% = .01 = \dfrac{1}{100}$ $25\% = .25 = \dfrac{25}{100}$

Remember...

Every percentage can be displayed as a percentage, a decimal, or a fraction with a denominator of 100.

Exercises   WRITE DECIMALS AND FRACTIONS

1 45% = _____ = _____
     (decimal)   (fraction)

2 35% = _____ = _____
     (decimal)   (fraction)

3 43% = _____ = _____
     (decimal)   (fraction)

4 10% = _____ = _____
     (decimal)   (fraction)

5 87% = _____ = _____
     (decimal)   (fraction)

6 2% = _____ = _____
     (decimal)   (fraction)

7 59% = _____ = _____
     (decimal)   (fraction)

8 .1% = _____ = _____
     (decimal)   (fraction)

9 .45% = _____ = _____
     (decimal)   (fraction)

10 Out of 100 questions, Yoshi answered 76 questions correct on his math exam. What percentage of questions did Yoshi answer correctly?

_____

11 Emily is dividing her birthday cake among 10 people. If each person receives an equal 10% of the cake, how could Emily use fractions to express a single piece of cake? How could she use decimals to express a single piece of cake?

_____

Name _____

Percents and Fractions

Since percents are ratios, you can change them to fractions. The denominator will be 100. The numerator will be the number in front of the percent sign.

Examples:

What is 40% of 50?

Step 1: Convert the percent to a fraction.
$$40\% = \frac{40}{100}$$

Step 2: Simplify the fraction if you can.
$$\frac{40}{100} = \frac{2}{5}$$

Step 3: Multiply $\frac{2}{5} \times 50 = \frac{100}{5}$

Step 4: Simplify the product. $\frac{100}{5} = \frac{20}{1} = 20$

You can also change fractions to percents. $\frac{3}{4} = ?\,\%$

Step 1: Divide 100 by the denominator.
$$100 \div 4 = 25$$

Step 2: Multiply the numerator by the product.
$$3 \times 25 = 75$$

Step 3: Add the percent sign. $\frac{3}{4} = 75\%$

Remember...

Some fractions *cannot* be changed easily to percents. If 100 cannot be divided evenly by the fraction's denominator, you will not be able to convert that fraction to a percent.

Exercises   CONVERT

Convert the percent to a fraction and reduce where possible.

1 35%   **2** 47%   **3** 25%   **4** 6%   **5** 91%

6 52.3%   **7** 2.05%   **8** 17%   **9** 49.5%   **10** .1%

Convert the fraction to a percent. Round to two digits to the right of the decimal.

11 $\frac{5}{8}$ **12** $\frac{1}{9}$ **13** $\frac{15}{16}$ **14** $\frac{3}{13}$ **15** $\frac{1}{10}$

16 $\frac{3}{200}$ **17** $\frac{5}{3000}$ **18** $\frac{5}{7}$ **19** $\frac{454}{1000}$ **20** $\frac{1}{400}$

Percents and Decimals

Because percents are really hundredths, a percent can always be changed to a decimal. But be careful!

Examples:

Change 3% to a decimal.

Step 1: Think: 3% = 3 hundredths.

Step 2: Write the correct decimal: 3% = .03

Decimals can also be changed to percents. The easiest way to do this is to move the decimal point two places to the right and add the percent sign.

Change .3925 to a percent.

Step 1: Move the decimal point two places to the right. 39.25

Step 2: Add the percent sign. So .3925 = 39.25%

Exercises   CONVERT

Convert the percent to a decimal. Round to four digits to the right of the decimal.

1 10%   2 67%   3 .02%   4 96.4%   5 55.32%

6 1110.01%   7 23.456%   8 .075%   9 34%   10 1003%

Convert the decimal to a percent. Round to two decimal places to the right of the decimal.

11 .03   12 1.02   13 .0027   14 .025   15 100.01

16 .145   17 .0101   18 .125   19 .0825   20 .009

Name _____

Multiplying Percents and Fractions

Since percents can be expressed as fractions, they can be multiplied as if they were fractions.

When finding a percent of a fraction, the answer will be a *fraction*.

Examples:

What is 24% of $\frac{5}{6}$?

Step 1: Change the percent to a fraction.

$$24\% = \frac{24}{100}$$

Step 2: Simplify the fraction if you can.

$$\frac{24}{100} = \frac{6}{25}$$

Step 3: Multiply the fractions. $\frac{6}{25} \times \frac{5}{6} = \frac{30}{150}$

Step 4: Simplify the product. $\frac{30}{150} = \frac{1}{5}$

Step 5: So 24% of $\frac{5}{6} = \frac{1}{5}$

When multiplying a fraction by a percent, the answer will be a *percent*.

Multiply: $\frac{2}{7} \times 35\%$

Step 1: Change the percent to a fraction. $\frac{35}{100}$

Step 2: Simplify the fraction if you can. $\frac{7}{20}$

Step 3: Multiply the fractions. $\frac{2}{7} \times \frac{7}{20} = \frac{14}{140}$

Step 4: Simplify the product. $\frac{14}{140} = \frac{1}{10}$

Step 5: Change the fraction to a percent. 10%

Exercises   MULTIPLY

Give the answer as a fraction.

1. 35% of $\frac{1}{6}$

2. 22% of $\frac{6}{7}$

3. 25% of $\frac{1}{4}$

4. 78% of $\frac{4}{5}$

5. 4% of $\frac{2}{3}$

6. 56% of $\frac{3}{7}$

7. 37% of $\frac{3}{13}$

8. 51% of $\frac{1}{8}$

9. 44% of $\frac{4}{9}$

10. 10% of $\frac{3}{17}$

Give the answer rounded to two digits to the right of the decimal point.

11. $\frac{3}{5}$ of 20.2%

12. $\frac{1}{11}$ of 37%

13. $\frac{3}{4}$ of 75.75%

14. $\frac{2}{3}$ of 66%

15. $\frac{1}{8}$ of 88.08%

16. $\frac{3}{13}$ of 152%

17. $\frac{3}{8}$ of 225%

18. $\frac{5}{6}$ of 11%

19. $\frac{2}{17}$ of 34.34%

20. $\frac{1}{4}$ of .024%

Unit Test

Lessons 8–12

In which place does the underlined number reside?

1 3,456.9<u>8</u>7 _____

2 5<u>3</u>9,992 _____

3 45.573.793<u>4</u> _____

4 <u>8</u>17,993 _____

Round.

5 Round 567,893.546 to the nearest hundredth. _____

6 Round 495,679.559 to the nearest ten thousand. _____

Convert decimals to fractions.

7 .85 = _____

8 .625 = _____

9 .06 = _____

10 .375 = _____

Convert fractions to decimals.

11 $\frac{4}{5}$ = _____

12 $\frac{4}{15}$ = _____

13 $\frac{7}{8}$ = _____

14 $4\frac{1}{8}$ = _____

Put the decimals in order from greatest to least.

15 .22, .45, .76, .765, .43, .432, .226, .89

_____

16 .117, .017, .033. .087, .243, .2043, .657, .0657, .0605

_____

Lessons 8–12

Add or subtract.

25   .57397
    + .3542

18   .034056
    + .43776

19   .564
      .667
   + .35832

20   4.5466
    − 1.2505

21   .792654
    − .600043

22   1.476
    − .78334

23 Gwen went to the store to buy supplies for school. She spent $1.50 on a pencil sharpener, $4.05 on a set of markers, $3.70 for a used compass, $3.09 for a memo pad, and $6.28 for a new water bottle. How much did she spend altogether?

_____

Calculate.

24   .3033
    ×   9

25   24.615
    ×   45

26   .873
    ×   15

27   .539
    ×   .98

28   .438
    ×   .64

29   .7784
    ×   .647

30 Jamie went to the store to buy lunch for his 6 friends. For each friend, he spent $4.75 for a sandwich, $1.25 for a cold beverage, and $.56 for a piece of fruit. How much did he spend in total to buy lunch for his friends?

_____

Unit Test

Lessons 8–12

Calculate.

31 $3\overline{)\,.9693}$

32 $23\overline{)\,15.387}$

33 $2.55\overline{)\,4.256715}$

34 $.23\overline{)\,.69092}$

35 $.025\overline{)\,.545}$

36 $.44\overline{)\,.3224672}$

37 $.215\overline{)\,.43043}$

38 $.25\overline{)\,124}$

39 Theo and his drama club raised a total of $1,563.75 for the local
Boys and Girls Club. There are 15 people in the drama club.
How much, per person, did the drama club raise? _____

40 What is 30% of $\frac{3}{5}$? _____

41 What is 40% of 240? _____

42 What is $\frac{3}{4}$ of 240%? _____

43 $\frac{5}{18}$ is what percentage of $\frac{25}{72}$? _____

44 What is $\frac{1}{3}$ of 42%? _____

45 What is $\frac{4}{5}$ of 90%? _____

46 What is 23% of .605? _____

47 What is 44% of .906? _____

Name _____

Exponents

An **exponent** tells how many times a number should be multiplied by itself. An exponent is usually written as a small number next to, and slightly above a number that is larger in size. The larger number is called the base of an exponent. Each exponent represents a "power." You have already learned about the powers of 10. 10^4 is 10 to the 4th power. Any number can be a base. 2^5 is 2 to the 5th power. 3^3 is 3 to the 3rd power.

$$2^5 = 2 \times 2 \times 2 \times 2 \times 2 = 32$$

$$4^2 = 4 \times 4 = 16$$

$$10^4 = 10 \times 10 \times 10 \times 10 = 10,000$$

$$3^3 = 3 \times 3 \times 3 = 27$$

Often, when the exponent is 2, people say "squared" instead of to the 2nd power. $4^2 = 4$ to the 2nd power = 4 squared. Remember that squared means "to the 2nd power."

You can add or subtract numbers with exponents.

Example: $3^4 - 5^2$

Step 1: Find the value of the first **exponential expression**:
$3^4 = 3 \times 3 \times 3 \times 3 = 81$

Step 2: Find the value of the second exponential expression:
$5^2 = 5 \times 5 = 25$

Step 3: Calculate: $81 - 25 = 56$

Exercises   FIND THE VALUE

1. 2^3
2. 5^2
3. 12^3
4. 4^3
5. 12^2

6. 2.5^2
7. 10^3
8. 7^4
9. 1.2^2
10. 5^4

11. 3^5
12. $(.01)^2$
13. 2^7
14. $(.05)^3$
15. 10^5

16. $(1.1)^2$
17. 7^3
18. 25^2
19. 30^3
20. $(.002)^3$

21. Jasper was planning to hand out flyers to his friends to spread the word about an upcoming charity event. He wanted to give his six friends enough flyers for them to each give a flyer to six of their own friends. How many flyers will Jasper need?

_____

22. Oren's dad offered him a choice of $13.00 total to buy eight newspapers, or 4 cents for the first newspaper, 8 cents for the second newspaper, 16 cents for the third newspaper, and so on up to the eighth newspaper. Which choice of payment should Oren take? Why?

_____

Scientific Notation

Scientific notation is a way to express any number as a decimal greater than 1, multiplied by a power of 10. For example: 3,500 can be expressed as 3.5×10^3 and 4,230,000 can be expressed as 4.23×10^6.

How do you find which power of ten to use? Look at the number in standard, or regular, notation. Place a decimal point at the far right of that number. Move the decimal point left until you create a number that is greater than 1 but less than 10. Then count the number of places you had to move the decimal point. That is the power of 10 to use for a particular number.

Remember...

When dropping zeros in a decimal, you may *not* drop any zero that has a number anywhere to its *right*. For example: In 4.00010, you may drop the final zero, but you may *not* drop the zeros between the 4 and the 1.

Example:

Express 530,200,000 in scientific notation.

Step 1: Place a decimal point at the *right* of the number. 530,200,000

Step 2: Move the decimal point to the *left* until you get a number that is greater than 1 but less than 10. The answer is 5.30200000

Step 3: Count the number of places you moved the decimal point. An easy way to do this is to count the number of places to the right of the decimal point. In this case, 8 places

Step 4: Drop all zeros at the *right* end of the number.

Step 5: Express the original number in scientific notation. 5.302×10^8

Exercises CONVERT TO SCIENTIFIC NOTATION

Round to six decimal places to the right of the decimal.

1. 125

2. 7,453

3. .0254

4. 37

5. .00457

6. 1,222,333

7. 898

8. 45.32

9. 190.325

10. 13,023

11. 5.567

12. 72.354

13. 4,777.77

14. .02002

15. 233.323

16. 5672

14.1

Name _____

Order of Operations

There are rules for which computations you do first, second, third, and so on. **Order of operations** is the set of rules that tells you what steps to follow when doing a computation. The order of operations is PEMDAS. These letters stand for:

Parentheses

Exponents

Multiplication and Division

Addition and Subtraction

Example:

$30 - 4 \times 6 + 12 \div 2^2 - (5 - 2) = ?$

We need to solve this problem using the **order of operations.**

Step 1: Solve the parts that are inside **parentheses.**
$(5 - 2) = 3$

Now you have this: $30 - 4 \times 6 + 12 \div 2^2 - 3 = 7$

Step 2: Rename the parts that have **exponents** in standard notation. $2^2 = 4$

So now you have: $30 - 4 \times 6 + 12 \div 4 - 3 = ?$

Step 3: Solve **multiplication** problems.
$4 \times 6 = 24$

The string is slowly becoming shorter!

Now you have $30 - 24 + 12 \div 4 - 3 = ?$

Step 4: Work any **division** problems.
$12 \div 4 = 3$

Again, this problem is starting to look even simpler.
$30 - 24 + 3 - 3 = ?$

Step 5: **Add** and **subtract** as you move along from left to right.

First, $30 - 24 = 6$. Then $6 + 3 = 9$.
Then $9 - 3 = 6$.

Do not group the additions separately from the subtractions, unless they are in parentheses!
Answer: $30 - (24 + 3) - 3 = 0$

Remember...

You can remember PEMDAS best if you make up a phrase. Here is one that may help: **P**eople **E**at **M**any **D**esserts **A**fter **S**chool!

Exercises SOLVE

1 $5 - (4 - 3) + 5 \times 4$

2 $(3 \times 2)^2 \times 2 - 2 + 4$

3 $(3 + 2)^2 \times 4 - 3 + \dfrac{4}{2}$

4 $5 - 7 + 4 \times 2 - 3$

5 $55 - 2 \times \dfrac{3}{2} - 10^2$

6 $(2 + 3 + 4)^{3-1}$

7 $(2 - 2)^2 + (4 - 2)^2$

8 $(3 - 4) + 3^2 \times 3 + 2$

9 $4 \times (11 - 7) - (44 + 28)$

72   Lesson 14.1   Order of Operations

Commutative and Associative Properties

Numbers behave in specific ways. Each kind of number behavior is called a **property**.

The Commutative Property of Addition: Addends may be added in any order without changing the sum. An **addend** is any number in an addition problem. It does not matter the order in which you add those numbers. The sum will always be the same.

The Commutative Property of Multiplication: Numbers may be multiplied in any order without changing the product.

The Associative Property of Addition: Addends may be grouped in any way without changing the sum.

The Associative Property of Multiplication: Numbers may be grouped in any way without changing the product.

Examples:
Find the answers to the following problems and tell which property they represent.

$26 + 41 + 10 = ?$ $10 + 26 + 41 = ?$
(Answers are 77 and 77, examples of the **commutative property**.)

$25 \times 2 \times 3 = ?$ $3 \times 25 \times 2 = ?$
(Answers are 150 and 150, examples of the **commutative property**.)

$(13 + 17) + 10 = ?$ $13 + (17 + 10) = ?$
(Answers are 40 and 40, examples of the **associative property**.)

$(5 \times 6) \times 3 = ?$ $5 \times (6 \times 3) = ?$
(Answers are 90 and 90, examples of the **associative property**.)

Exercises IDENTIFY THE PROPERTY

1 $3 \times 4 \times 2 = 2 \times 4 \times 3$
_____

2 $1 + 9 + 22 = 22 + 9 + 1$
_____

3 $2 + 3 + 3 + 2 = 2 + (3 + 3) + 2$
_____

4 $4 \times 2 + 2 \times 3 = 2 \times 4 + 3 \times 2$
_____

5 $7 \times 2 \times 7 = 7 \times (2 \times 7)$
_____

6 $7 \times 7 \times 8 \times 7 = 8 \times 7 \times 7 \times 7$
_____

7 $(9 + 7) + 6 = 9 + (7 + 6)$
_____

8 $4 \times 5 \times 5 \times 4 = 5 \times 5 \times 4 \times 4$
_____

9 $2 + 6 + 8 + 3 = 6 + 3 + 8 + 2$
_____

10 $(6 \times 4) \times 2 = 6 \times (4 \times 2)$
_____

11 $12 + 13 + 13 + 12 = 12 + 12 + 13 + 13$
_____

12 $7 \times 8 + 8 \times 7 = 8 \times 7 + 8 \times 7$
_____

Name _____

Distributive Property and Identity

The Distributive Property of Multiplication: When you multiply numbers, you may multiply by each separately, and then add their products.

> **Example:**
>
> $7 \times (3 + 1) = (7 \times 3) + (7 \times 1)$
>
> $28 = 21 + 7$

Multiplication and division are closely related. When you learned how to divide fractions, you were shown that division is the same thing as multiplication by a reciprocal. You can use the Distributive Property of Multiplication when you are dividing. But you may only use the Distributive Property when the addends are in the dividend.

Identity elements are numbers in a problem that do not affect the answer.

When adding, the identity element is 0. Any addend or addend + 0 will not change the total. In multiplication, the identity element is 1. Any factor or factors × 1 will not change the product. Subtraction and division do *not* have identity elements.

Remember...

You cannot use the Distributive Property when addends are in the divisor.

$90 \div (2 + 3)$ *does not* $= (90 \div 2) + (90 \div 3)$ *because* . . .

$(90 \times \frac{1}{5})$ *does not* $= (90 \times \frac{1}{2}) + (90 \times \frac{1}{3})$

18   *does not* =   45   +   30

Exercises   IDENTIFY THE PROPERTY

1 $0 + 5 = 5$

_____

2 $5 (4 + 3) = 5 \times 4 + 5 \times 3$

_____

3 $15 + 0 = 15$

_____

4 $2 (3 + 2 + 3) = 2 \times 3 + 2 \times 2 + 2 \times 3$

_____

5 $20 \times 1 = 20$

_____

6 $24 + 0 = 24$

_____

7 $2 \times 3 + 2 \times 7 = 2 (3 + 7)$

_____

8 $\frac{(7 + 6)}{4} = \frac{7}{4} + \frac{6}{4}$

_____

9 $34 + (0 + 2) = 34 + 2$

_____

10 $45 (3 + 2 + 0) = (45 \times 3) + (45 \times 2) + (45 \times 0)$

_____

11 $0 + 4 = 4 + 0$

_____

12 $7 (23 - 14) = 7 \times 23 - 7 \times 14$

_____

Name _____

14.4

Zero Property, Equality Properties

Learning these properties will make your mathematics work easier.

Did you ever try to multiply by 0? The answer is 0.

Zero Property of Multiplication: Any number $\times 0 = 0$.

Remember that an equation is a mathematical statement that two things are equal.
$5 + 3 = 2 + 6$

Equality Property of Addition: If you add a number on one side of an equation, you must add *the same number* on the other side of the equation. Both sides will then still be equal.
$(5 + 3) + 7 = (2 + 6) + 7$

Equality Property of Subtraction: If you subtract a number on one side of an equation,

you must subtract *the same number* on the other side of the equation. Both sides will then still be equal.
$(5 + 3) - 1 = (2 + 6) - 1$

Equality Property of Multiplication: If you multiply one side of an equation by a number, you must multiply the other side of the equation by *the same number*. Both sides will then still be equal.
$(5 + 3) \times 9 = (2 + 6) \times 9$

Equality Property of Division: If you divide one side of an equation by a number, you must divide the other side of the equation by *the same number*. Both sides will then still be equal. **But you may never divide by 0.**
$(5 + 3) \div 4 = (2 + 6) \div 4$

Exercises   IDENTIFY THE PROPERTY

1. $5 \times 0 = (4 + 1) \times 0$

_____

2. $\dfrac{(8 \times 1)}{2} = \dfrac{(4 + 4)}{2}$

_____

3. $(2 + 3) \times 0 = 0$

_____

4. $7(0 + 0) = 0$

_____

5. $(7 \times 4) + 0 = (14 \times 2) + 0$

_____

6. $123.45 \times 0 = 0$

_____

7. $(12 \times 6) - 5 = (9 \times 8) - 5$

_____

8. $15 \times 4 = (3 \times 5) \times 4$

_____

Answer yes or no.

9. If $6 + 2 = 4 + 4$ then does $4(6 + 2) = 4(4 + 4)$? _____

10. If $5 \times 8 = 4 \times 10$ then does $\dfrac{(5 \times 8)}{4} = \dfrac{(4 \times 10)}{4}$? _____

11. If $2 \times 12 = 3 \times 8$ then does $4 - 2 \times 12 = 3 \times 8 - 4$? _____

12. If $10 \times 8 = 4 \times 20$ then does $10 \times 8 - 2.53 = 4 \times 20 - 2.53$? _____

13. If $\dfrac{3}{4} = \dfrac{12}{16}$ then does $\dfrac{3}{4} - 5 = \dfrac{12}{16} - 5$? _____

Name _____

Understanding Variable Expressions

Sometimes you want to solve a problem to find an unknown number. The unknown number is called a **variable**. Variables are usually expressed as letters. Variables are used with numbers and symbols in **algebra**, a kind of math used to find the value of unknowns. An **algebraic expression** is a group of letters, numbers, and operations.

Examples:	$n + 19$	$(p - 72) \times 3$
$(36 \div g) + 9$	$\dfrac{b}{3}$	$12 \times m$

When you have a variable in a multiplication expression, you do not need to use the $\times$ symbol. So $12 \times m$ is usually written as $12m$. The 12 is called a **coefficient**, which is a number that multiplies a variable.

Exercises   EXPRESS

Write each expression in word form.

1 $\dfrac{b}{6}$

_____

2 $x + 4$

_____

3 $2d + 10$

_____

4 $5q - 5$

_____

5 $\dfrac{(z - 5)}{33}$

_____

6 $(3h + 4)\, 10$

_____

7 $2p - 3$

_____

8 $14\, (p - 22)$

_____

9 $(22 - 3)\, j + 2$

_____

10 $10u - 3u$

_____

11 $\dfrac{9y}{(10y - 2)}$

_____

12 $\dfrac{1}{2}f + \dfrac{1}{4}f$

_____

Solving Equations by Addition and Subtraction

You learned the Equality Properties of Addition and Subtraction, which say that if you add or subtract a number to one side of an equation, you must add or subtract the same number to the other side of the equation. This rule is important when you are trying to solve equations that use addition and subtraction.

Examples:

Problem: $z - 32 = 51$. Find z.
Can you add 32 to the left side of the equation to leave z by itself? You can do that, but you also have to add 32 to the right side of the equation.

Step 1: Add the same number to both sides of the equation. $z = 51 + 32$

Step 2: Add $51 + 32 = 83$. So $z = 83$

Problem: $d + 9 = 21$. Find d.
This time, you can subtract 9 from the left side of the equation to leave d by itself. But you have to subtract 9 from the right side of the equation, too.

Step 1: Subtract the same number from both sides of the equation. $d = 21 - 9$

Step 2: Subtract $21 - 9 = 12$. So $d = 12$

Exercises SOLVE

1. $w + 3 = 10$

2. $12 = q + 8$

3. $2 + y = 34$

4. $7 - e = 4$

5. $s + 17 = 50$

6. $d - 4 = 11$

7. $z + 10 = 25$

8. $23 = 5 + r$

9. $m + 45 = 54$

10. $15 + t = 33$

11. $45 - g = 30$

12. $3 - f = 1$

13. $45 + r = 71$

14. $21 = 45 - u$

15. $26 + r = 49$

16. $v + 5 = 91$

Name _____

Solving Equations by Multiplication and Division

Before you begin to solve equations by multiplication and division, you should review some interesting things about numbers.

Division is the "opposite" of multiplication. Multiplication is the "opposite" of division. If you multiply an original number by a second number, and then divide the product by the second number, you are left with the original number. For example: $3 \times 5 \div 5 = 3$. If you divide an original number by a second number, and then multiply the quotient by the second number, you will be left with the original number. For example: $6 \div 3 \times 3 = 6$. That works because division is the same as multiplying by a reciprocal.

Examples:

$$3 \times 5 \div 5 = 3 \times \left(5 \times \frac{1}{5}\right) \qquad 5 \times \frac{1}{5} = \frac{5}{5} = 1$$

$$6 \div 3 \times 3 = 6 \times \left(\frac{1}{3} \times 3\right) \qquad \frac{1}{3} \times 3 = \frac{3}{3} = 1$$

Remember...

In an equation, you need to treat both sides in the same way. Whatever you do to one side, you must also do to the other side.

You know that if you have a fraction with the same number in the numerator and denominator, the fraction is equal to 1. So $\frac{5}{5} = 1$, $\frac{3}{3} = 1$, and $\frac{w}{w} = 1$. (You do not even need to know the value of w!)

Examples:

Problem: $\frac{k}{5} = 12$. Solve for k.

Since $\frac{k}{5} = k \times \frac{1}{5}$, you multiply the left side of the equation by 5. Then you would have $k \times 1$, which is equal to k alone. You can multiply the left side by 5 *only* if you *also* multiply the right side by 5.

Step 1: Multiply both sides by the same number.
$k = 12 \times 5$

Step 2: Multiply: $12 \times 5 = 60$. So $k = 60$

Problem: $7u = 56$. Solve for u.
Now, you divide the left side by 7 to get u. You must also divide the right side by 7.

Step 1: $u = 56 \div 7$

Step 2: Divide: $56 \div 7 = 8$. So $u = 8$

Exercises SOLVE

1 $3x + 10 = 19$

2 $4 + 7m = 32$

3 $10b + 8 = 118$

4 $12 + 2p = 88$

5 $\frac{y}{7} = 49$

6 $10 + 2u = 14 + u$

Negative Numbers

Negative numbers are numbers that are less than zero. You identify them by adding a minus sign to the front of a number. So -1 is 1 less than 0. -53.5 is 53.5 less than 0.

Example:

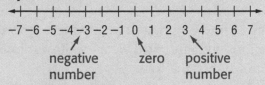

negative   zero   positive
number   number

Look at the number line. Notice that -3 is three spaces to the left of 0 on the negative side. Also

note that 3 is three spaces to the right of 0 on the positive side.

The Property of Additive Inverses: When you add a negative number to its **inverse** (its exact opposite on the other side of the number line), the total is 0. For example, $-7 + 7 = 0$.

Exercises SOLVE

1 $(-8) + 8 =$

_____

2 $(-134) + 134 =$

_____

3 $(-12) + 13 + 11 + (-13)$

_____

4 $100 + (-100) =$

_____

5 $20 + (-17) =$

_____

6 $(-65) + 65 + 61 + (-58) =$

_____

7 $\frac{1}{2} + \left(-\frac{1}{2}\right) =$

_____

8 $212 + 200 + (-212) + (-212) =$

_____

9 $31 + (-34) + 0 =$

_____

10 $76 + \frac{1}{4} + \left(-\frac{1}{4}\right) + (-76) =$

_____

11 Is -6 to the left or the right of -6.2 on the number line?

_____

12 Is -4.5 greater or less than -4.0?

_____

Adding with Negative Numbers

When you add a positive number and a negative number, compare the numbers as if they do not have positive or negative signs. If the positive number is larger, just subtract.

Example:

$6 + (-4) = ?$

Step 1: Remove the $+$ sign and the parentheses.

Step 2: Do the math. $6 - 4 = 2$

If the negative number is greater, ignore the minus sign for the time being. Subtract the smaller number from the greater. Then put a minus sign in front of the difference.

Example:

$1 + (-3) = ?$

Step 1: Subtract: $3 - 1 = 2$

Step 2: Write a minus sign in front of the difference. So $1 + (-3) = -2$

When adding two negative numbers, ignore the minus sign and **add**. Then write a minus sign in front of the total.

Example:

$(-1) + (-6) = ?$

Step 1: Ignore the negative signs and add.
$1 + 6 = 7$

Step 2: Write a minus sign in front of the total.
$(-1) + (-6) = -7$

Exercises   SOLVE

1 $12 + (-4)$

2 $(-14) + 8$

3 $3 + (-13)$

4 $45 + (-23)$

5 $123 + (-43) + 22$

6 $90 + (-45) + (-3)$

7 $(-10) + (-10) + 3$

8 $45 + (-32) + 2$

9 $15 + (-14)$

10 $16 + 14 + (-13)$

11 $(-15) + 14$

12 $67 + 12 + 13 + (-14)$

13 $43 + (-32) + 5$

14 $(-43) + 32 + (-5)$

15 $2 + 2 + (-3) + (-2)$

16 $4 + (-5) + 5$

17 $21 + (-45)$

18 $45 + (-43)$

Name _____

Plotting Ordered Pairs

The figure on the right is a **grid**. A grid has a horizontal axis, known as the *x*-axis, and a vertical axis, known as the *y*-axis. All points on a grid can be expressed, or identified, by two numbers: the *x*-coordinate, which indicates where the point is located on the *x*-axis and the *y*-coordinate, which indicates where the point is located on the *y*-axis. Each point is identified using the *x* and *y* coordinates in an **ordered pair**.

The point where the vertical and horizontal axes meet is the **origin**. The origin is identified by the ordered pair (0,0). The *x*-coordinate indicates how far the point is to the right (positive) or to the left (negative) of the origin. The *y*-coordinate indicates how far the point is above (positive) or below (negative) the origin.

Example:

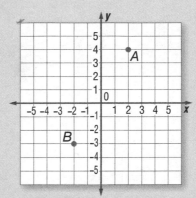

To find the *x*-coordinate, move your finger along the *x*-axis to the point. To find the *y*-coordinate, move your finger along the *y*-axis to the point. To identify the ordered pair, put the two coordinates in parentheses—the first number is the *x*-coordinate and the second number is the *y*-coordinate. In this figure, point A can be expressed as A(2,4) and point B can be expressed as B(−2,−3).

Exercises   **GIVE ORDERED PAIRS**

1 Give the ordered pair for each point on the graph.

A _____   B _____

C _____   D _____

E _____   F _____

G _____   H _____

I _____   J _____

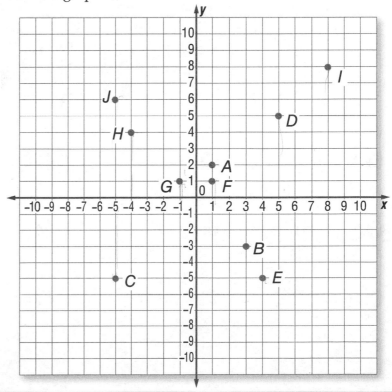

16.3

Exercises   **PLOT ORDERED PAIRS**

Plot the ordered pairs on the graph.

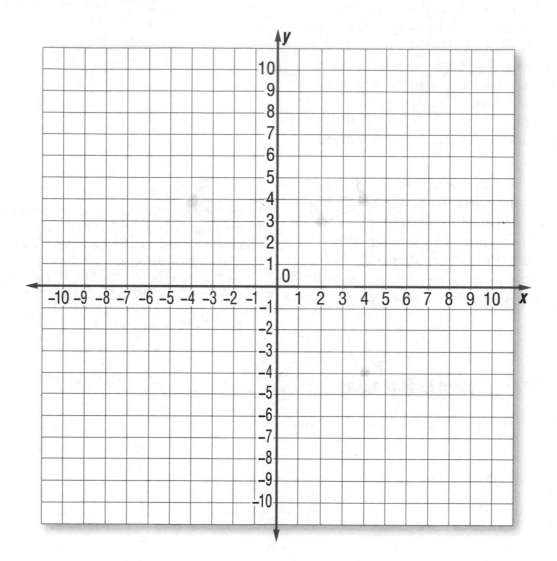

1 A (2,3)　　　　**2** B (4,−4)　　　　**3** C (4,4)　　　　**4** D (−4,4)

5 E (−4,−4)　　　　**6** F (5,2)　　　　**7** G (8,2)　　　　**8** H (8,6)

9 J (−5,6)　　　　**10** K (3,−4)　　　　**11** L (−2,−2)

Unit Test

Lessons 13–16

Restate in exponential form, then calculate.

1 $2 \times 2 \times 2 \times 2 + 3 \times 3 \times 3$ _____

2 $4 \times 4 \times 4 \times 4 - 5 \times 5 \times 5$ _____

3 $2 \times 2 \times 2 \times 2 \times 2 \times 2 + 6 \times 6 - 5 \times 5$ _____

Restate using scientific notation.

4 3,456,984.01 _____

5 8,694.1 _____

6 .00945 _____

7 1,094,659,041 _____

8 63.56 _____

Calculate using order of operations (PEMDAS).

9 $3 \times (6 - 4)^2 + (15 - 5) \times 5 + (5 - 3) \times 4 + 3^3$ _____

10 $17 - (9 + 5) + (5 - 3) \times 2 + (9 - 4)^2$ _____

11 $24 + (3 + 5) \times 5 + (6 - 3)^2$ _____

12 $33 - (4 - 2)^3 + 6 \times 2 + (5)^2 - 3$ _____

What number property does each expression display?

13 $3 + 4 + 5 = 5 + 4 + 3$ _____

14 $3(4 + 6) = 3(4) + 3(6)$ _____

15 $(15 + 16) + 18 = 15 + (16 + 18)$ _____

16 $34(1) = 34$ _____

17 $3 + 0 = 3$ _____

18 $16(5 - 3) = (16 \times 5) - (16 \times 3)$ _____

Lessons 13–16

19 $15 \times 5 = 5 \times 15$ _____

20 $33(0) + (33 + 0) = 0 + 33 = 33$ _____

21 $(7 \times 4) \times 20 = 7 \times (4 \times 20)$ _____

Solve for x.

22 $4 + x = 7$ **23** $x - 5 = 12$ **24** $29 - x = 25$

25 $x + 30 = 90$ **26** $4x + 5 = 13$ **27** $3x - 5 = 13$

28 $5x + 4 = 39$ **29** $3x + 4 = 28$ **30** $-4x + 4 = -28$

31 $\frac{x}{4} + 5 = 25$ **32** $\frac{x}{2} - 5 = 30$ **33** $\frac{2}{3}x - 4 = 26$

Solve the equation and indicate the point on the number line that corresponds with the answer.

```
        C   B A  D
 ←+―+―+―●―+―●―+―●―+―●―+―+―+―+―+―+―+―+―+―+―+―+―+―+→
  -10 -9 -8 -7 -6 -5 -4 -3 -2 -1  0  1  2  3  4  5  6  7  8  9 10
```

34 $-8 + 10 - 5$ _____   **35** $-10 + 5 + 4$ _____

36 $-8 + (-5) + 8$ _____   **37** $7 - 5 + (-10)$ _____

Lessons 13–16

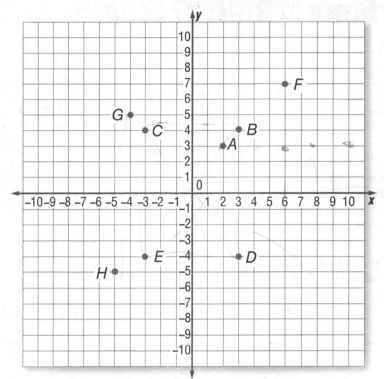

Provide the ordered pairs for the points plotted on the graph.

38 A _____ **39** B _____ **40** C _____ **41** D _____

42 E _____ **43** F _____ **44** G _____ **45** H _____

46 Plot the following points on the grid provided.

A(4,4)

B (8,4)

C(8,7)

D(−5,5)

E(−3,−8)

F(4,−7)

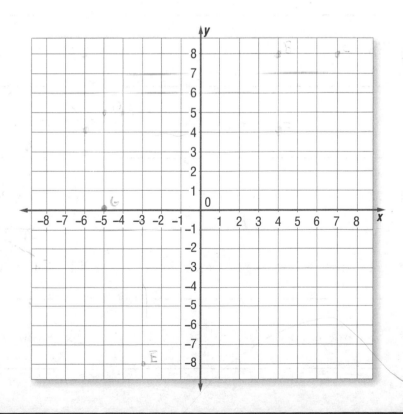

Name _____

Customary Units of Length

The customary units of length are inches (in.), feet (ft), yards (yd), and miles (mi).

1 foot = 12 in.
1 yard = 3 ft
1 mile = 1,760 yd

You can compare these units to each other.

Remember...

You do *not* have to add the plural *s* when you abbreviate units of measure.

Example:

How many feet are in a mile?

Step 1: You know that there are 3 feet in a yard, so multiply the number of yards × 3.

Step 2: 1,760 × 3 = 5,280. There are 5,280 feet in a mile.

Exercises   **CONVERT**

1 3.5 feet is how many inches?

_____

2 2 miles is how many feet?

_____

3 39 inches is how many yards?

_____

4 5 miles is how many feet?

_____

5 78 inches is how many feet?

_____

6 10,000 yards is how many miles?

_____

7 10.5 yards is how many feet?

_____

8 7.25 miles is how many inches?

_____

9 3.75 yards is how many inches?

_____

10 125 miles is how many yards?

_____

11 72 feet is how many miles?

_____

12 72 feet is how many inches?

_____

13 245 yards is how many feet?

_____

14 10,000 inches is how many miles?

_____

15 53 yards is how many miles?

_____

16 9,000 yards is how many inches?

_____

Customary Units of Liquid Volume

Liquid volume is the amount of liquid a container can hold. The customary units of liquid volume are cups (c), pints (pt), quarts (qt), and gallons (gal).

1 pint = 2 c
1 quart = 2 pt
1 gallon = 4 qt

You can compare these units to each other.

Example:
How many cups are in a gallon?

Step 1: You know that there are 4 quarts in a gallon, and there are 2 pints in a quart. So multiply the number of quarts × 2 to find out how many pints are in a gallon.

Step 2: 4 × 2 = 8 pints in a gallon.

Step 3: You know that there are 2 cups in a pint. So multiply the number of pints × 2.

Step 4: 8 × 2 = 16 cups in a gallon.

Exercises CONVERT

1 1 gallon is how many pints?

_____

2 A 23-gallon gas tank holds how many quarts?

_____

3 54 quarts is how many gallons?

_____

4 15 pints is how many gallons?

_____

5 1,000 cups is how many quarts?

_____

6 250 pints is how many cups?

_____

7 57 gallons is how many pints?

_____

8 21 quarts is how many cups?

_____

9 32 pints is how many gallons?

_____

10 88 pints is how many quarts?

_____

11 125 cups is how many pints?

_____

12 125 pints is how many cups?

_____

13 77 gallons is how many quarts?

_____

14 22 pints is how many gallons?

_____

15 256 quarts is how many gallons?

_____

16 256 pints is how many gallons?

_____

Name _____

Customary Units of Weight

The **customary units of weight** are ounces (oz), pounds (lb), and tons.

1 pound = 16 oz

1 ton = 2,000 lb

You can compare these units to each other.

> **Example:**
> How many ounces are in three pounds?
> **Step 1:** You know that there are 16 oz in one pound. So multiply the number of ounces in one pound by three.
> **Step 2:** $16 \times 3 = 48$ ounces in three pounds.

Exercises CONVERT

1 10 pounds is how many ounces?

_____

2 15.2 tons is how many pounds?

_____

3 14 tons is how many ounces?

_____

4 125 ounces is how many pounds?

_____

5 .234 tons is how many pounds?

_____

6 1 pound is how many tons?

_____

7 .892 tons is how many ounces?

_____

8 14 ounces is how many pounds?

_____

9 32 tons is how many pounds?

_____

10 2,345 ounces is how many tons?

_____

11 45.2 lbs is how many ounces?

_____

12 60,000 ounces is how many tons?

_____

13 A 250-pound man weighs how many tons?

_____

14 A 3.5-ton elephant weighs how many pounds?

_____

15 A $\frac{3}{4}$ ton truck can carry $\frac{3}{4}$ of a ton of materials. How many pounds is that?

_____

16 If there are 850 students at school and each eats 4 ounces ($\frac{1}{4}$ pound) of hamburger for lunch, how many pounds of hamburger, in total, do the students eat every day?

_____

Name _____

Perimeter

Sometimes you want to know the **perimeter**. The perimeter is the distance around a figure. To find the perimeter of a figure, add the lengths of all of its sides.

Examples: The perimeter of this triangle is $6 + 8 + 10 = 24$ in.

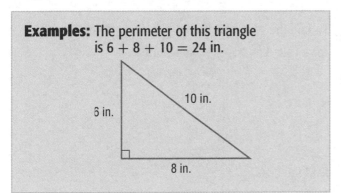

Find the figure's perimeter.

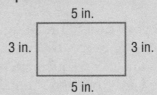

Step 1: Add the lengths of all sides.
$5 + 3 + 5 + 3 = 16$

Step 2: Write your answer using the correct unit.
16 in.

Step 3: If you need to, you can change the unit to a larger or smaller one. Since 12 inches = 1 foot, you can change the answer into feet by dividing by 12.

Step 4: $16 \div 12 = \dfrac{16}{12}$

Step 5: You may simplify the fraction and change it into a mixed number.
$\dfrac{16}{12} = \dfrac{4}{3} = 1\dfrac{1}{3}$
So the perimeter of the rectangle is $1\dfrac{1}{3}$ ft.

Exercises   SOLVE

1 What is the perimeter of a 2-inch square?

_____

2 A right triangle with sides measuring 3, 4, and 5 feet has what perimeter?

_____

3 Which has a longer perimeter, a 7-foot square or a rectangle with sides of 5 feet and 8 feet?

_____

4 A farmer is building a fence and wants to save fencing material. So he builds a rectangular fence with sides of 30 feet and 45 feet. One of the shorter sides of the fence will be the side of the barn. How many feet of fencing material will the farmer need?

_____

5 Which has a longer perimeter, a 14-foot square or an equilateral triangle with sides of 10 feet?

_____

6 A triangle has one side of 5 inches and two sides of 7 inches. What is its perimeter?

_____

7 A triangle has 3 equal sides of 200 feet. What is its perimeter?

_____

8 A building has a rectangular base with sides of 200 feet and 450 feet. What is its perimeter?

_____

Name _____

Area

Sometimes you want to find a figure's **area**, or the number of units it would take to fill it. Those units are called square inches or square feet, square yards, or even square miles.

> **Remember...**
>
> Be careful! A square foot *does not equal* 12 square inches. It equals 144 square inches. A square yard *does not equal* 3 square feet. It equals 9 square feet.

Examples:

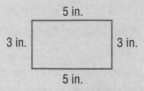

To find the area of a rectangle or a square, multiply the length × the width. In a rectangle and a square, both lengths and both widths are the same, but use only *one* of *each* when you multiply.

Area = 5 in. (length) × 3 in. (width) = 15 square inches.

To find the area of a triangle, multiply its length (also called its base) × its height × $\frac{1}{2}$.

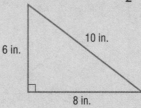

Find the area.

Multiply $6 \times 8 \times \frac{1}{2} = 24$ square inches.

Exercises   SOLVE

1 What is the area of a square with 4 ft sides?

_____

2 If a rectangle has sides of 2 ft and 12 ft, what is its area?

_____

3 There are 9 sq ft in one square yard (3 ft × 3 ft). How many square feet are in a 3-yd by 4-yd rug?

_____

4 How much will the area decrease if you take away 3 feet from each side of a square with 10-ft long sides?

_____

5 John walks west 20 ft, then 10 ft to the south, then 20 ft to the east, and then returns to his starting point to form a rectangle. What is the area of that rectangle?

_____

6 If a square that has sides of 25 ft is split in half, what is the area of each of the pieces?

_____

7 A right triangle has sides of 7 ft, 24 ft, and 25 ft. What is its area?

_____

8 Which has a larger area, a triangle with a base of 15 ft and a height 25 ft or a square with sides of 14 ft?

_____

17.6

Volume of a Solid

You learned the units for measuring liquid volume in a container. However, if you want to know how many units a solid figure contains, or its **volume**, the units are called cubic inches, cubic feet, or cubic yards.

Example:

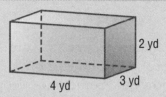

2 yd
4 yd   3 yd

To find the volume of a rectangular solid, multiply its length × its width × its height.

Volume = 4 × 3 × 2 = 24 cubic yards

Exercises SOLVE

1 A football field measures 360 ft long and 165 ft wide. If a construction company is told that they need to have 3 feet of gravel under the field for proper drainage how many cubic yards do they need to order?

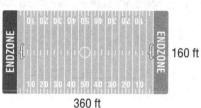

160 ft

360 ft

_____

2 A shoe box has dimensions of 12 inches by 10 inches by 7 inches. How many cubic inches is it?

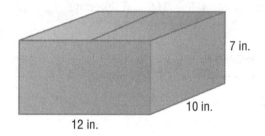

7 in.

10 in.

12 in.

_____

3 What is the volume of a cube with sides of 5 ft?

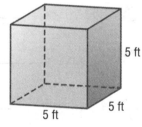

5 ft
5 ft
5 ft

_____

4 A shipping box has dimensions of 6 in. by 5 in. by 8 in. If a pound of granola takes up a cubic inch, how many pounds of granola can you put in the box?

_____

5 A rectangular solid with sides of 8 ft by 4 ft by 11 ft has what volume?

_____

6 A cube that has sides of 216 inches has how many cubic yards of volume?

_____

Time

You already know most of the units of time. They are seconds, minutes, hours, days, weeks, months, and years. Sometimes people also talk about decades and centuries.

1 minute = 60 seconds

1 hour = 60 minutes

1 day = 24 hours

1 week = 7 days

1 month = 28 or 29 or 30 or 31 days. (Months can vary in length. Some have 30 days, while others have 31. February has only 28 days, except in a leap year when it has 29.)

1 year = 12 months = 52 weeks = 365 days. (A leap year has 366 days. The extra day is added to February.)

a decade = 10 years   a century = 100 years

Example:

How many days are in a three-year span of time that has a leap year?

Add 2 times 365 + 366 = 1,096 days

Remember...

To speak accurately about time, you need to know two other terms.

a.m. = *ante meridiem*, which means "before the middle of the day." So a.m. hours are between midnight and noon.

p.m. = *post meridiem,* which means "after the middle of the day." So p.m. hours are between noon and midnight.

Exercises   SOLVE

1 24 hours = _____ seconds

2 35 days = _____ hours

3 365 days = _____ minutes

4 12 hours = _____ days

5 52 weeks = _____ days

6 51 hours = _____ minutes

7 24 days = _____ weeks

8 200 years = _____ decades

9 3,000 years = _____ centuries

10 42 days = _____ minutes

11 2 weeks = _____ seconds

12 45 minutes = _____ hours

13 If you got paid $800 and you worked 2.92 days, approximately how much did you make per hour?

_____

14 How much do you have to pay a rock band that will play for 2 hours that wants to be paid $15/second?

_____

15 3 decades = _____ hours
Assume 365 days per year.

16 A man tells you he is 2,270,592,000 seconds old. How many years old is he if you assume 365 days per year?

_____

Temperature

The unit of temperature is the degree. It is written as a small circle above the number. 65° = 65 degrees.

Customary degrees are measured on the Fahrenheit scale. However, there are other scales, so you must add the letter **F**, or the

word Fahrenheit, to make it clear that you are measuring on the customary scale.

65° F = 65 degrees Fahrenheit.

In customary units, the freezing point of water is 32° F. The boiling point of water is 212° F.

Exercises   CONVERT

For this exercise F will be the symbol for the temperature in degrees Fahrenheit. C will be for the temperature in degrees Celsius. To convert from one scale to the other you use one of the following formulas:

$(F - 32) \times (\frac{5}{9}) = C$ and $C \times (\frac{9}{5}) + 32 = F$

1   32° F = _____ C

2   100° C = _____ F

3   −149° F = _____ C

4   0° C = _____ F

5   100° F = _____ C

6   72° F = _____ C

7   32° C = _____ F

8   212° C = _____ F

9   40° F = _____ C

10   120° F = _____ C

11   50° C = _____ F

12   50° F = _____ C

13   5° C = _____ F

14   −10° F = _____ C

15   −10° C = _____ F

16   −30° C = _____ F

Name _____

Metric Units of Length

The metric units of length are millimeters (mm), centimeters (cm), meters (m), and kilometers (km)

1 centimeter = 10 mm

1 meter = 100 cm

1 km = 1000 m

You may have noticed that metric units are based on the powers of 10. So they are easy to work with. For example: 1 meter = 1000 mm = 100 cm = .001 km.

Remember...

Learn these prefixes:

milli = thousandth

centi = hundredth

kilo = thousand

Examples:

How many cm = 35 m?

Step 1: Think: 100 cm = 1 m

Step 2: Multiply the number of meters × 100.

You can do this by regular multiplication.
35 × 100 = 3500

However, it is much easier to move the decimal point two places to the right.

35 m = 3500 cm

How many m = 465 mm?

Step 1: Think: 1000 mm = 1 m

Step 2: Divide: $465 \div 1000 = \frac{465}{1000}$

You can also do this calculation by moving the decimal point three places to the left.

456 mm = .456 m

Exercises   CALCULATE

① 235 cm = _____ m

② 4235 mm = _____ m

③ 5.7 km = _____ cm

④ 625 km = _____ mm

④ 235 cm + 300 mm = _____ m

⑥ 1.6 km = _____ cm

⑦ 5 cm + 5 mm = _____ m

⑧ 3.87 m = _____ mm

⑨ 5 km + 50 m = _____ m

⑩ 200 km + 200 m = _____ cm

⑪ 400 cm = _____ km

⑫ 25 m + 10 cm = _____ cm

⑬ 45 m + .25 m = _____ mm

⑭ 11 km = _____ m

⑮ 33 cm + 33 mm + 33 m = _____ m

⑯ 57 m = _____ km

Metric Units of Liquid Volume

The basic metric unit of liquid volume is the **liter** (L). There are also milliliters (mL), centiliters (cL), and kiloliters (kL).

You can probably figure out that:

1 liter = 1000 mL

1 kiloliter = 1000 liters

Example:
How many milliliters are in 3.5 liters?

Step 1: Think: 1000 mL = 1 liter

Step 2: Multiply: 1000 by 3.5 = 3500 mL

Remember...

All metric units are powers of 10.

Exercises   CALCULATE

1   1.1 L = _____ mL

2   700 L = _____ kL

3   .56 L = _____ mL

4   35 L = _____ mL

5   3 kL = _____ mL

6   21 mL = _____ L

7   457 mL = _____ kL

8   77 mL + 77 L = _____ L

9   1 kL + 35 L = _____ L

10   41 mL + 41 L = _____ kL

11   4 kL − 325 L = _____ L

12   35 kL + 3500 L = _____ kL

13   23 L + .23 mL = _____ L

14   41 L − 23 mL = _____ mL

15   If a water cooler holds 30 liters of water, and each cup of water holds 250 milliliters, how many cups can you fill before the water cooler is empty?

_____

16   If there are 35 students and each expects to drink 10 half-liter bottles of water in a week, how many many total liters is this?

_____

17   A half-liter bottle of soda is a common size. How many bottles of soda would it take to fill a 10-liter container?

_____

18   If a reservoir holds 100,000,000 liters of water, then how many kiloliters of water does it hold?

_____

Name _____

Metric Units of Mass

The basic metric unit of mass is the **gram** (g). There are also milligrams (mg), centigrams (cg), and kilograms (kg).

Since you know about metric prefixes, you could probably make the following list yourself!

1 cg = 10 mg

1 g = 100 cg

1 kg = 1000 g

Example:

How many grams are in an object that has a mass of 4.25 kilograms?

Step 1: Think: 1000 grams = 1 kilogram

Step 2: Multiply: 4.25 × 1000 = 4250 grams

Exercises   CALCULATE

1. 100 g = _____ kg

2. 15 kg = _____ mg

3. 550 g = _____ kg

4. 5600 mg = _____ g

5. 1.1 kg = _____ mg

6. 100 mg = _____ g

7. 400 g + 300 mg = _____ g

8. 3 kg + 200 g = _____ cg

9. 550 g + .32 kg = _____ g

10. 10 kg − 233 g = _____ kg

11. 45 g − 200 mg = _____ g

12. 3300 g + 1100 mg = _____ kg

13. 2200 g − 340 mg = _____ g

14. 2.3 kg + .66kg = _____ g

15. 1 mg + 1 g + 1 kg = _____ kg

16. 15 g − 15 cg − 15 mg = _____ g

17. 42 g + 100 mg = _____ cg

18. 35 g + 3500 g = _____ kg

19. 100 kg − 2100 g = _____ kg

20. 33 g + 33 cg + 33 mg = _____ g

Perimeter, Area, and Volume of a Solid: Metric

You can calculate perimeters, areas, and volumes of solids using metric units of length. You perform *exactly* the same kinds of calculations you do when you are working with customary units of length. The only difference is that when you work with metric units, your answers will be expressed in metric units.

Perimeter is expressed in mm, cm, m, or km.

Area is expressed in square mm, square cm, square m, or square km.

Volume of a solid is expressed in cubic mm, cubic cm, cubic m, or cubic km.

When writing metric volume, you may also use the abbreviation cu. instead of writing out the whole word cubic.

Remember...

When you calculate the area of a figure or the volume of a solid, do not change units from one kind to another. For example, 1 cu km *does not equal* 1000 cu m.

Exercises   SOLVE

1 What is the perimeter of a 5-meter square?

_____

5 m

2 What is the area of a rectangle with sides of 27 km and 1.1 km?

1.1 km
27 km

_____

3 A cube with sides of 2 m has what volume?

_____

2 m
2 m
2 m

4 A square with sides of 1.2 m has an area of how many sq cm?

_____

1.2 m

5 A cube with sides of 3.6 km has a volume of how many cubic meters?

_____

3.6 km
3.6 km
3.6 km

6 What is the area of a triangle with a base of 11 m and a height of 18 m?

_____

18 m
11 m

7 A rectangular prism has a base of 3 m by 10 m and a height of 4 m. What is its volume?

_____

8 What is the volume of air for 500 m above a field that is 300 m by 400 m? State you answer in cubic kilometers.

_____

9 Rita walks 5 km to the east before walking 4 km to the north. She then turns to the west and walks 5 km. How many kilometers will she have to walk to return to her starting point. What was her total distance in meters?

_____

_____

10 Calculate the volume, in cubic meters, of a swimming pool with a level bottom. It is in the shape of a rectangle with sides of 15 m by 9 m, and with a depth of 3 m.

15 m

9 m

_____

11 What is the area of a triangle with base of 10 m and a height of 8 m?

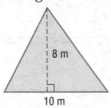

8 m

10 m

_____

12 What is the volume of a rectangular solid that is 2 km by 13 km by 8 km?

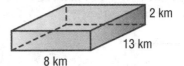

2 km

13 km

8 km

_____

13 If you are traveling at 100 kph, how many meters would you travel in 15 minutes?

_____

14 What is the area of a rectangle with sides of 4 m and 7 m?

_____

15 A carpet store charges by the square meter for carpet, and the store rounds up to the next square meter. How much carpet should be ordered for a room that is 5.5 m by 7.1 m?

_____

16 Jim is calculating how much dirt he will have to haul away when he digs a hole for the foundation of a house. He knows that a dump truck can carry 6 cubic meters of dirt at a time. The hole for the house is going to be 10 m by 7 m and 2 m deep. How many truck loads will he be filling?

_____

Changing from Customary Units to Metric Units

Use the chart below to help you convert customary units to metric units. The values may not be exact in all cases, but your answers will be close to correct.

Milk and fruit juices in the United States often include labels that express their liquid volume in **fluid ounces**. 1 fluid ounce = 29.574 milliliters.

Length	Liquid Volume	Weight
1 inch = 2.54 centimeters	1 cup = 0.237 liters	1 ounce = 28.35 grams
1 foot = 0.305 meters	1 pint = 0.473 liters	1 pound = 0.454 kilograms
1 yard = 0.914 meters	1 quart = 0.946 liters	1 ton = 907.18 kilograms
1 mile = 1.609 kilometers	1 gallon = 3.785 liters	

Remember...

A zero is often placed in front of a decimal point to avoid confusion. The zero does not change the value of the number that follows the decimal point!

Example:

3 yards = how many millimeters?

Step 1: Find yards on the chart above.
1 yard = 0.914 meters.

Step 2: Multiply $0.914 \times 3 = 2.742$

Step 3: Multiply meters $\times$ 1000 to find millimeters.
$2.742 \times 1000 = 2742$

So 3 yd — about 2742 mm.

Exercises   CALCULATE

1 3 feet is how many meters?

_____

2 A $\frac{1}{2}$ gallon is how many liters?

_____

3 Which is larger, a 16-ounce soda bottle, or a $\frac{1}{2}$ liter soda bottle?

_____

4 A 200-pound person weighs how many kilograms?

_____

5 If the highway exit sign says it is 2 miles to the next exit, how many kilometers is that?

_____

6 Which race should take longer, the 100-yard or 100-meter dash?

_____

7 If a tank has a 105.68 gallon capacity, how many liters is that?

_____

8 Which is heavier, a 16-ounce steak or a .5-kilogram steak?

_____

9 A 2-ton truck weighs how many kilograms?

_____

10 If a man is 6.56 feet tall, how many meters tall is he?

_____

Name _____

Changing from Metric Units to Customary Units

Use the chart below to help you convert metric units to customary units. The values may not be exact in all cases, but your answers will be close to correct.

Length	Liquid Volume	Weight
1 millimeter = 0.039 inches	1 liter = 1.056 quarts	1 gram = 0.035 ounces
1 centimeter = 0.394 inches	1 kiloliter = 263.2 gallons	1 kilogram = 2.205 pounds
1 meter = 39.37 inches		
1 kilometer = 0 .621 miles		

Example:

4 meters = *about* how many feet?

Step 1: Find meters on the chart above.
1 meter = 39.37 inches

Step 2: Multiply 39.37 × 4 = 157.48 inches

Step 3: Divide inches by 12 to find feet.
157.48 ÷ 12 = 13.1225 feet

So 4 meters = *about* 13.1233 feet.

You might be asked to round this to the nearest whole number. 4 meters = *about* 13 feet

Exercises   CALCULATE

1. Which is larger, a 2-liter bottle of soda or a 2-quart bottle?

   _____

2. A 2-meter long snake is how many inches long?

   _____

3. A man weighs 91 kilograms. How many pounds is that?

   _____

4. The police officer said that you were traveling at a speed of 100 kilometers an hour. How many miles per hour were you traveling?

   _____

5. The weight limit on a bridge is 15,000 kilograms. How many tons is that?

   _____

6. 100 meters is how many yards?

   _____

7. Is $5.00 a gallon for gas more than $1.75 a liter?

   _____

8. 7 liters of water is about how many quarts?

   _____

9. Which is shorter, 15 millimeters or .75 inches?

   _____

10. Which is larger, a 200 gram steak or a $\frac{1}{2}$ pound one?

    _____

Lessons 17–19

Solve.

1 Wilfredo is replacing the trim around all of the windows in his house.
The perimeter of each window measures 124 inches and he has 9 windows.

How many feet of trim does Wilfredo need to replace? _____

2 Ainsley wants to fill a fish tank with water for her new fish. The fish tank
holds 176 quarts and she is adding the water with a one-gallon container.

How many gallon containers will she need to fill the tank? _____

3 Tom is weighing potted plants for shipping to customers. The first plant weighs
1670 ounces, the second plant weighs $100\frac{1}{8}$ pounds, and third plant weighs
one twentieth of a ton.

Which plant weighs the most? _____

Which plants weighs the least? _____

4 Sally wants to build a fence in her garden to keep the rabbits out, and she
needs to know how much fencing to buy. The garden has an irregular shape
with sides of $15\frac{1}{4}$ feet, 660 inches, 12 yards, one foot, $\frac{1}{160}$ of a mile, and 6 feet.

How much fence material does she need (in feet)? _____

5 What is the area of a rectangle with a length of 20 ft
and a width of 144 inches? _____

6 What is the area of a right triangle with lengths of
3 feet, 4 feet, and 60 inches? _____

7 What is the volume of a rectangular box with sides of 24 inches, and
$1\frac{1}{2}$ feet, and a height of 18 inches? _____ cubic feet

8 A modern spacecraft travels 4.9 miles per second to maintain enough
speed to stay in orbit around the earth. How far does the spacecraft travel

in a minute? _____

in an hour? _____

in a day? _____

Lessons 17–19

9 If the earth is 24,000 miles in circumference, how much time would it take the spacecraft in Exercise 8 to orbit the earth once? _____

How many times a day would the spacecraft orbit the earth? _____

How many times in a week? _____

How many times in a year? _____

10 The world record for the high jump is 2.45 meters. The world record for the pole vault is 6.14 meters. How many centimeters higher is the pole vault record than the high jump record? _____

11 Stacy is measuring fabric for her grandmother, who is going to make a rectangular banner for a parade float. The banner will be 4.5 meters in length and 1,350 millimeters in width.

How much fabric is needed for the banner? _____ sq cm

12 Heidi has three cans of cooking oil to recycle. One can holds 1,456 milliliters of oil, the second can holds 23.4 centiliters of oil, and the third can holds 4.5 liters of oil.

How much cooking oil is Heidi going to recycle? _____ liters

13 What is the area of a triangle with sides of 6 cm, 6 cm, a base of 9 cm, and a height of 4 cm? _____ sq cm

14 Jerold walked around the rectangular school gymnasium, which measures 56 meters by 6,500 centimeters. How many meters did Jerold walk? _____

15 How much corn feed can fit into a rectangular bin that measures 4.6 meters in width, 14.5 meters in length, and 5.5 meters high?

_____ cu meters

16 The average player on the basketball team is 6 feet 4 inches tall.

About how tall is that in centimeters? _____

17 The average US car has a gas tank that holds 65 liters of gasoline.

How much is that in gallons? _____

Name _____

Lessons 17–19

18 Paulie was looking for lawn mowing jobs. He surveyed the people in his neighborhood and found out that the average lawn measured 54 feet by 30 feet.

What is the total area in square feet? _____

In square yards? _____

About how much is the total area in square meters? _____

19 Normal body temperature is 98.6° F. What is that in Celsius? _____

20 The oil company suggests that people set the temperature in their homes at between 20 and 22 degrees Celsius during the winter.

What is that range in Fahrenheit? _____

21 What is the volume of the rectangular solid?

_____

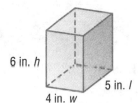

6 in. *h*

5 in. *l*

4 in. *w*

22 What is the volume of the triangular solid?

_____

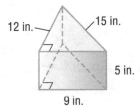

12 in.

15 in.

5 in.

9 in.

23 In track and field, the standard middle distance event is the 1,500 meters.

About how many feet is 1,500 meters? _____

About how much farther beyond 1,500 meters would someone have to run

in order to reach a mile? _____ feet

about _____ meters

24 The distance of a flight from New York to Phoenix, Arizona is about 2,400 miles. The average ground speed for a commercial airliner is about 850 kilometers per hour.

About how much time will it take to fly from New York to Phoenix?

_____ hours

Name _____

Points and Lines

A **point** is a specific location in space. It has no dimensions, and you cannot measure it. Since it would be impossible to see anything with no dimensions, we usually represent a point with a dot. Points are usually identified by a capital letter.

$$\overset{\bullet}{A} \qquad \overset{\bullet}{B}$$

A **line** is a straight path that goes in both directions and never ends. It has only one dimension, length. However, when we draw a line, it actually has a tiny bit of width—the width of a pencil point—or we would not be able to see it! A line can be identified by any two points located anywhere on it.

$$\overset{\bullet}{A} \qquad \overset{\bullet}{B}$$

You can identify a line in either direction. Line $\overleftrightarrow{AB}$ = Line $\overleftrightarrow{BA}$.

Some lines intersect. **Intersecting lines** cross each other at a specific point. Line $\overleftrightarrow{AB}$ and Line $\overleftrightarrow{CD}$ intersect at Point E.

> **Remember...**
>
> A line extends in *both* directions. It does not come to an end in *either* direction. Its only dimension is length.

Exercises   SOLVE

1 Use a symbol to name this figure.

_____

2 Identify the following figure.

$$\overset{\bullet}{M}$$

_____

3 Using symbols, give two names for this figure.

_____

4 Is the following figure a line? Explain your answer.

_____

_____

5 What is the point of intersection in this figure?

_____

6 Is AY a line? Explain your answer.

_____

_____

Name _____

Line Segments and Rays

A **line segment** is a specific part of a line. It ends at two identified points.

A line segment is named by its two end points. segment $\overline{FG}$ = segment $\overline{GF}$. $\overline{FG} = \overline{GF}$

A **ray** is a part of a line that extends from a specific point in only one direction. The specific point of a ray is called a **vertex** or an **endpoint**.

However, to identify a ray, you must use one other letter along the line's path.

Ray $\overrightarrow{HI}$ *does not equal* ray $\overleftarrow{IH}$, because the first point named in a ray shows the vertex, and ray $\overleftarrow{IH}$ goes in the opposite direction of ray $\overrightarrow{HI}$.

Exercises   SOLVE

1 For the figure below, call the point of intersection of the diagonals E. List all the line segments in the figure.

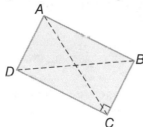

_____

_____

2 For the figure below, count how many line segments there are. Do not include line segments that contain another point. For example, the line segment $\overline{EH}$ contains the point I.

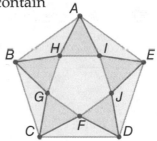

_____

_____

3 Name two rays from the image below.

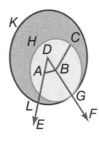

_____

_____

4 List three rays that contain the point N.

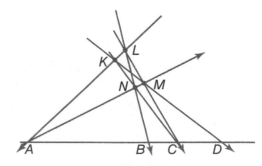

_____

_____

21.1

Name ______________________________

Measuring Angles

An **angle** is formed by the rays of two intersecting lines, when the rays have the same vertex. An angle is named by both of its lines, with the vertex *in the middle* of its name.

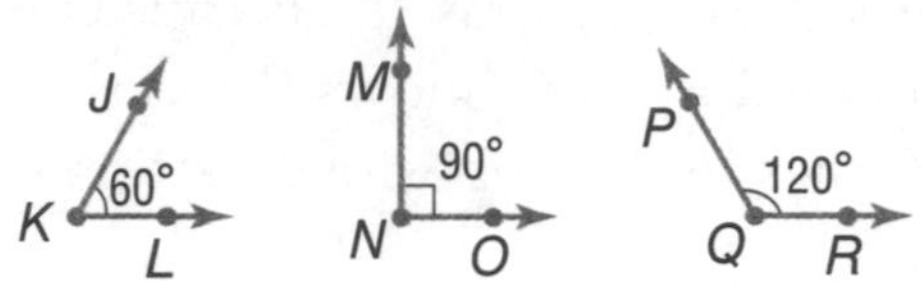

Rays KJ and KL intersect at Point K, a shared vertex, to form angle JKL.

Angles are measured in degrees. A straight line is 180°, so an angle will always be less than that. Angles that are less than 90° are called **acute angles**. Angles that are more than 90° are called **obtuse angles**. Angles that are *exactly* 90° are called **right angles**. Right angles are often indicated with a very small square at the point where the two lines meet.

In the angles shown on the left:
Angle JKL is an acute angle. Angle MNO is a right angle. Angle PQR is an obtuse angle.

Exercises **IDENTIFY**

1. Is the angle acute or obtuse?

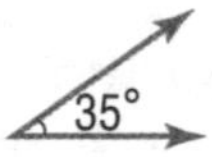

____

2. Is the angle acute or obtuse?

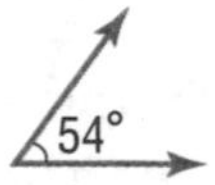

____

3. Is the angle acute, obtuse, or right?

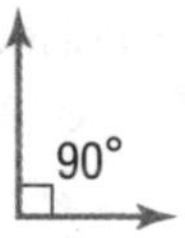

____

4. Is the angle acute, right, or obtuse?

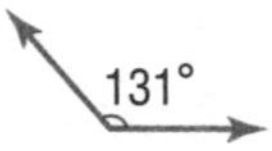

____

5. Is the angle acute, right, or obtuse?

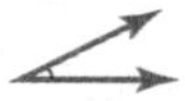

____

6. How many degrees do you need to subtract from the angle to make it acute?

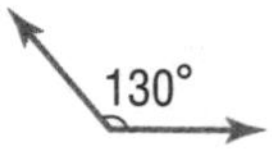

____

7. How many more degrees would you have to add to the angle to make it an obtuse angle?

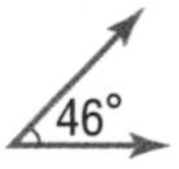

____

8. Can you subtract one obtuse angle from another and still have an obtuse angle?

____

9. What three angles below could you add together and not get an obtuse angle?

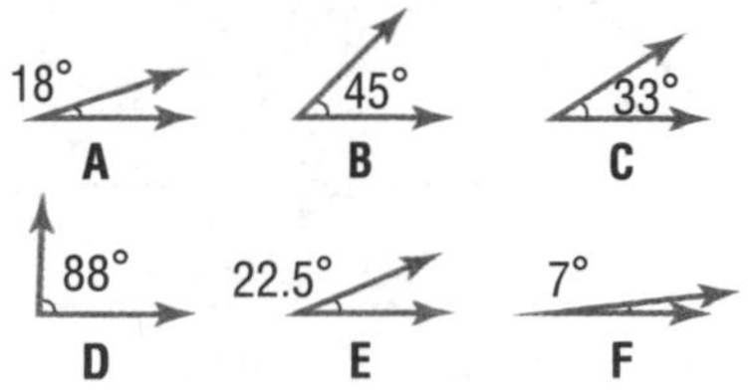

____

10. Are either of the angles below a right angle?

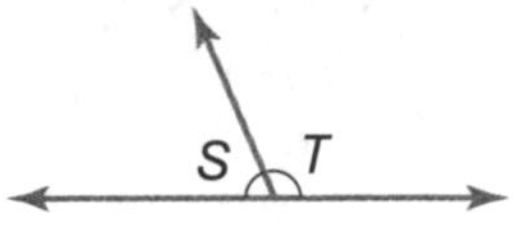

____

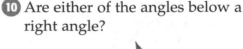

Types of Angles

Sometimes, two angles can be defined by their relationship to each other.

Supplementary angles are two angles that form a line. Their sum will be 180°, so if you know the measure of one, you can figure out the other. Note that angles can sometimes be called by just one letter, placed near the vertex.

Example:

If angle S = 113°, what is the measure of angle T?

Step 1: Think: A straight line = 180°

Step 2: Subtract: 180 − 113 = 67
So angle T = 67°

Remember...

You can easily *prove* that vertical angles are equal. Angle W and angle X form a straight line. So angle W = 180° − angle X. Angle Y and angle X also form a straight line. Angle Y = 180° − angle X. So angle W = angle Y!

Complementary angles are two angles that form a right angle. Their sum will be 90°.

Example:

If angle U = 32°, what's the measure of angle V?

Step 1: Think: A right angle = 90°

Step 2: Subtract: 90 − 32 = 58
So angle V = 58°

When two lines intersect, the angles opposite each other are called **vertical angles**.

Those angles are equal.

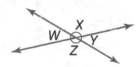

Exercises   IDENTIFY

1 Are the two angles shown below supplementary?

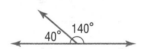

_____

2 Are the two angles below complementary?

_____

3 Are the two angles A and B supplementary?

_____

4 Are the two angles supplementary?

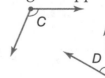

_____

5 Are the two angles CFD and DFE complementary? Why, or why not?

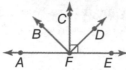

_____

6 Name the two angles below, and determine if they are supplementary.

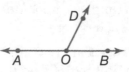

_____

7 Determine if the two angles are complementary.

_____

8 What size angle would you have to add to make this a right angle?

_____

9 In the figure below, list three sets of vertical angles.

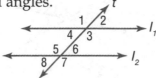

_____

10 Of the angles labeled below, which ones are supplementary?

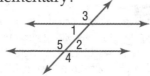

_____

11 List two pairs of vertical angles in the figure.

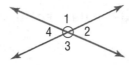

_____

12 What type of angles are C and B?

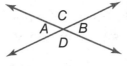

_____

13 List two pairs of vertical angles in the figure below.

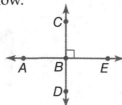

_____

14 What are the two angles in the figure below? Are the angles complementary? Assume that angle ACB is 90 degrees.

_____

Triangles

A 2-dimensional figure with three sides is a triangle. A triangle has three angles that *always* add up to 180°. This is one way that you can classify triangles.

A triangle with *only* acute angles—angles less than 90°—is called an **acute triangle**. A triangle with one right angle is called a **right triangle**. A triangle with one obtuse angle is called an **obtuse triangle**.

acute triangle   right triangle   obtuse triangle

Since the measures of the angles in a triangle add up to 180°, a triangle can have at most

only one right angle or one obtuse angle. Can you figure out why? Ask yourself: How many degrees are in two right angles? What is the smallest number of degrees that two obtuse angles could total?

Another way of thinking about a triangle is to look at the length of its sides. If all three sides are the same length, the triangle is **equilateral**. If two sides are the same length, but the third is different, the triangle is **isosceles**. And if all three sides have different lengths, the triangle is **scalene**.

equilateral triangle   isosceles triangle   scalene triangle

Exercises   IDENTIFY

Determine if the triangle is acute, right, or obtuse.

1

A 82°, C 61°, 37° B

_____

2

C, B, A

_____

3

115°

_____

Determine if the triangle is isosceles, equilateral, or scalene.

4

4 cm, 4 cm, 4 cm

_____

5
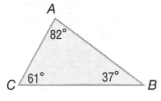
9 cm, 9 cm

_____

6
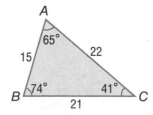
A 65°, 15, 22, B 74°, 21, 41° C

_____

22.2

Name _____

Quadrilaterals

A **quadrilateral** is a 2-dimensional figure with four sides – and four angles.

A **rectangle** has four right angles and two sets of opposite sides that are parallel, and equal in length. The lengths of the sides that meet at the right angle are not equal.

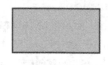

rectangle   square

A square is a special kind of rectangle. *All* of its sides are of equal length.

A **rhombus** does *not* have four right angles. However, like a rectangle, both sets of opposite sides are parallel and have the same length.

A **trapezoid** has two parallel sides, while the other two sides are not parallel to each other.

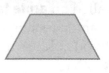

rhombus   trapezoid   kite

A **kite** looks like a typical toy kite. Two angles in a kite are equal. Two *touching* sides are equal in length, and the other two *touching* sides are equal in length.

Exercises   IDENTIFY

Determine what type of shape the figure is: square, rectangle, rhombus, trapezoid, or kite.

1
1.2 yd
1.2 yd   1.2 yd
1.2 yd

_____

2
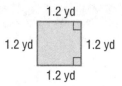

_____

3
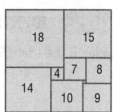
18	15
4	7	8
14	10	9

_____

4
A _____ B
D _____ C

_____

5
6 cm
3 cm   3 cm
11 cm

_____

6
D 5 cm
A   C
5 cm
B

_____

7
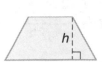
h

_____

8
E
H ⟨100°   40°⟩ F
G

_____

9
1
1   q
1   1
p
1

_____

Polygons

A **polygon** is any closed 2-dimensional figure that is made up of line segments. Triangles and quadrilaterals are polygons. However, a polygon can have any number of sides greater than 2. The number of sides = the number of angles. Many polygons are named for the number of sides.

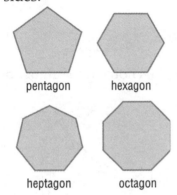

pentagon   hexagon

heptagon   octagon

penta = 5, **hexa** = 6, **hepta** = 7, **octa** = 8

Two polygons are **congruent** if their shape and size are the same. The sides and angles in one polygon must exactly equal the sides and angles in the other. Congruent polygons do *not* have to face in the same direction. The best way to find out if two polygons are congruent is to measure the sides and angles of both.

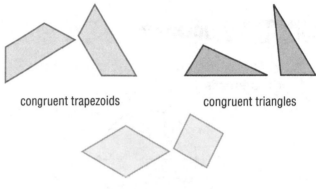

congruent trapezoids   congruent triangles

not congruent rhombuses

Exercises   IDENTIFY

Determine if the figure is a pentagon, a hexagon, a heptagon, or an octagon.

1

_____

2

_____

3

_____

4

_____

5

_____

6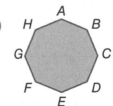
108°

_____

7
A B C D E F G H

_____

8

_____

9 Are these two figures congruent?

120°   60° 60° 60°

_____

10 Are these two figures congruent?

_____

Name _____

Circles

A **circle** is a 2-dimensional figure with every point on its circumference an equal distance from its center point, or **origin**. A circle's **circumference** is its perimeter, the distance around it.

A line segment that starts at a circle's origin and extends to its circumference is called a

radius. The plural of radius is **radii**. In a circle, all radii are equal in length.

A **chord** is a line segment that has both endpoints on the circumference. A **diameter** is a special kind of chord that passes through the origin. It is always equal in length to 2 radii.

Exercises   IDENTIFY

1 What is the radius of the circle, if the diameter is 11 cm?

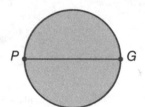

_____

2 Identify the chord in the figure below.

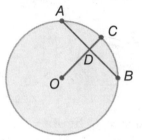

_____

3 Identify the 2 radii below.

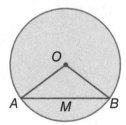

_____

4 What are the 5 chords formed by inscribing the pentagon inside of the circle?

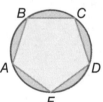

_____

5 Describe the two line segments from the connected points on the circle.

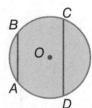

_____

6 Identify the diameter.

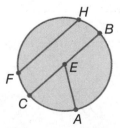

_____

Circles (cont.)

A circle's circumference and area are calculated by using a special long decimal, written as the Greek letter π, pronounced **pi**. To make calculations easier, pi is often rounded to 3.14. Pi is the ratio of a circle's diameter to its circumference—a ratio that is exactly the same for every circle.

Calculating the circumference and area of a circle is actually fairly easy to do. A circle's circumference = pi times its diameter (πd). A circle's area = pi times the square of its radius (π r²).

> **Example:**
>
> If a circle has a radius of 3 inches, you can find its circumference by multiplying the radius × 2 and then multiplying that number × π.
> Its circumference = (2 × 3) π inches
> = 6π = 18.84 inches
>
> To find this circle's area, you have to raise its radius to the second power and then multiply that times π. In this example, its area = (3 × 3) times π square inches = 9 times π = 28.26 square inches.

Exercises CALCULATE

1 Calculate the circumference of the circle below. Use 3.14 for π.

_____

2 Calculate the area of the circle below. Use 3.14 for π.

_____

3 Calculate the area and circumference of the circle below. Use 3.14 for π.

_____

4 Calculate the area and circumference of the circle below. Use 3.14 for π.

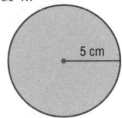

_____

5 Calculate the area and circumference of the circle below. Use 3.14 for π.

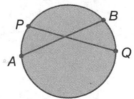

_____

6 Name the two chords that have been drawn in the figure below.

_____

Name _____

Solid Figures

A **solid figure** is a figure that has 3 dimensions. These are some common solid figures:

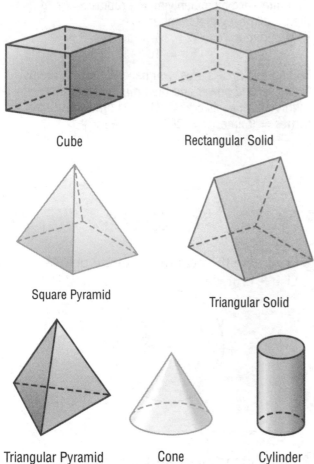

Cube   Rectangular Solid

Square Pyramid   Triangular Solid

Triangular Pyramid   Cone   Cylinder

Here are some terms that are used to describe solid figures:

Face: The flat surface of a solid figure. Each face looks like a 2-dimensional figure.

Edge: The line where two faces meet.

Vertex of a Solid: A specific point at which *more than* 2 faces meet, or a point where a curve begins.

Base: The face on the bottom of a solid figure.

Examples:

Look at the solid figures drawn on this page.

A cube and a rectangular solid have 6 faces each. Any of the bases can be the base.

A square pyramid has 5 faces. The base is square and the other 4 faces are triangular.

A triangular solid has 5 faces. Two of them are triangular. Three are rectangular.

A cone has a circular base and 1 vertex. A cylinder has 2 circular faces and *no* vertex.

A triangular pyramid has a triangular base, 4 vertices, 4 faces, and 6 edges.

Exercises   IDENTIFY

1 How many faces does this figure have?

2 How many faces does this figure have?

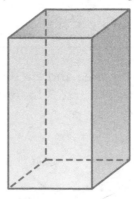

_____   _____

3 What shape is the base of this figure?

_____

4 How many faces does this figure have?

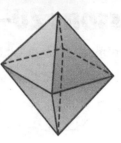

_____

5 How many edges does this solid have?

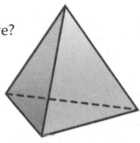

_____

6 How many faces does this solid have?

_____

7 How many vertices does this solid have?

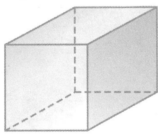

_____

8 How many vertices does this solid have?

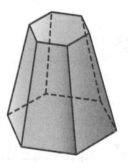

_____

9 How many edges does this solid have?

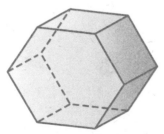

_____

10 How many edges and vertices does this cube have?

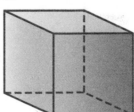

_____

Unit Test

Lessons 20–22

Identify each angle as obtuse, acute, or right.

1  128°
_____

2 90°
_____

3 55°
_____

4 35°
_____

5 101°
_____

Identify each pair of angles as supplementary or complementary, and explain why.

6
_____

7
_____

8
_____

Identify each triangle as scalene, equilateral, or isosceles.

9
_____

10
_____

11
_____

12
_____

13
_____

14
_____

Lessons 20–22

Identify each triangle as obtuse, right, or acute.

15 _____

16 _____

17 _____

18 _____

19 _____

20 _____

21 _____

22 _____

23 _____

24 _____

25 _____

26  _____

Identify the following quadrilaterals.

27 _____

28 _____

29  _____

30

Lessons 20–22

31 Name the center point. _____

32 Which segments are chords? _____

33 Which segment is the diameter? _____

34 Which segments are radii? _____

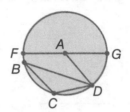

Identify each figure and fill in the information requested.

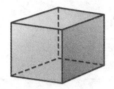

35

Figure _____
Base is _____
Number of faces _____
Number of edges _____
Number of vertices ____

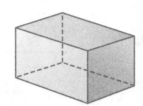

36

Figure _____
Base is _____
Number of faces _____
Number of edges _____
Number of vertices ____

37

Figure _____
Base is _____
Number of faces _____
Number of edges _____
Number of vertices ____

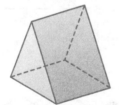

38

Figure _____
Base is _____
Number of faces _____
Number of edges _____
Number of vertices ____

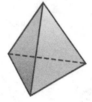

39

Figure _____
Base is _____
Number of faces _____
Number of edges _____
Number of vertices ____

40

Figure _____
Base is _____
Number of faces _____
Number of edges _____
Number of vertices ____

41 Figure _____
Base is _____
Number of faces _____
Number of edges _____
Number of vertices ____

Bar Graphs

Graphs are useful ways to display information, or **data**. A **bar graph** uses bars to compare two or more people, places, or things. The bars in this type of graph may be horizontal or vertical, but not both. Each bar represents a number. Because the data are shown visually, the bars can be compared to one another. Sometimes, different colored bars that represent different kinds of people or things are used.

Examples:

Each student at Centertown Middle School voted for his or her favorite kind of pie.

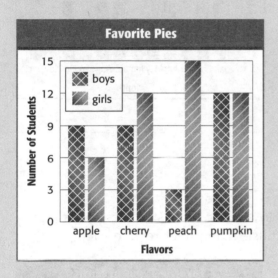

The key tells you that the bars that are cross-hatched stand for boys and the bars with slashes stand for girls. The horizontal line, or **axis**, at the bottom of the graph names different kinds of pie. The vertical axis tells you how many boys and how many girls voted for that kind of pie.

How many students voted for either apple or peach?

Step 1: Find "apple" on the horizontal axis. Look at the top of each bar in the "apple" section, and follow that line back to the vertical axis to find out how many girls voted for apple pie, and how many boys voted for apple pie. 9 boys + 6 girls = 15 students voted for this kind of pie.

Step 2: Find "peach" on the horizontal axis. Repeat the process.
3 boys + 15 girls = 18 students

Exercises   INTERPRET

❶ Use the graph below to identify the second most-liked fruit.

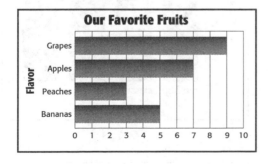

_____

❷ According to this bar graph, what was the least favorite color for students' favorite juices?

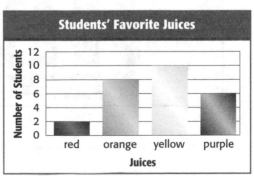

_____

3 Ignoring "Other," what is the least common means for students to get to school according to the bar graph below?

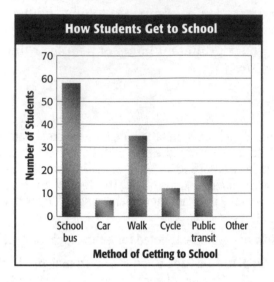

How Students Get to School

_____

4 A class survey asked each student his or her birth month. The graph below displays this data. What month had the most student birthdays?

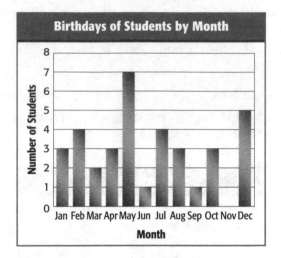

Birthdays of Students by Month

_____

5 Which Canadian province has the third highest Average Annual Income?

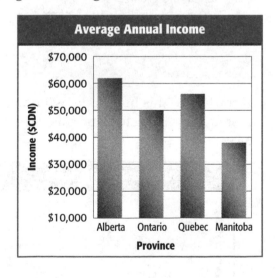

Average Annual Income

_____

6 How many more students prefer jazz music than prefer rock music?

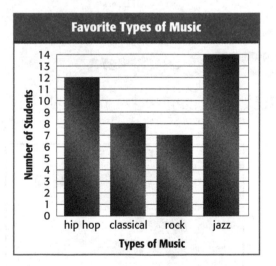

Favorite Types of Music

_____

Line Graphs

A **line graph** often shows how information changes as time passes. Each number on the horizontal axis represents a specific time. The distance from one time to another is called an **interval**. In a line graph, the steeper a line segment is, the more change there has been during that interval.

Example:

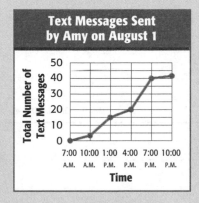

Text Messages Sent by Amy on August 1

During what interval did Amy send the most messages? About how many messages did she send during that interval?

Step 1: Look for the steepest line segment between intervals. That segment is between 4:00 P.M. and 7:00 P.M.

Step 2: Look along the horizontal axis for the time at the beginning of that interval. Then look at where the line is at that time on the vertical axis to find out how many text messages Amy sent by then. By 4:00, Amy had sent 20 text messages.

Step 3: Look for the time at the end of that interval. Find out how many text messages Amy had sent by then. By 7:00, Amy had sent 40 messages.

Step 4: Subtract. 40 − 20 = 20. So between 4:00 and 7:00, Amy sent 20 text messages.

Exercises INTERPRET

1 Between what two years did the number of dolphin sightings increase the most?

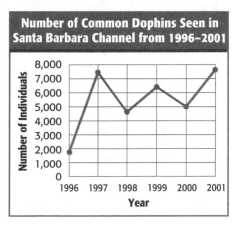

Number of Common Dolphins Seen in Santa Barbara Channel from 1996–2001

_____

2 What number of students could locate materials in 20 minutes?

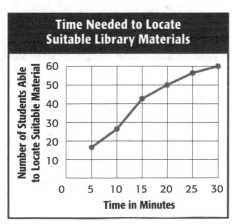

Time Needed to Locate Suitable Library Materials

_____

3 Looking at the line graph below, what two days would you try to avoid going to the Registration office?

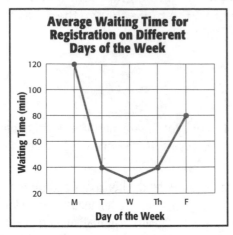

_____

4 Between what two days did you learn the most?

_____

5 What are the two most popular days for consuming potatoes, according to the line graph?

_____

_____

How many kilos of potatoes are consumed on those two days?

_____

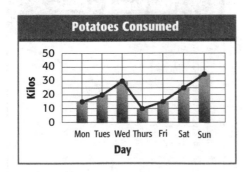

6 From the line graph below, describe the levels of ozone between January and March.

_____

_____

Name _____

Double-Line Graphs

A **double-line graph** often compares how information changes *for two or more* people, places, or things as time passes.

Example:

When did Amy and Jim both send exactly the same total number of messages? How many total messages did each of them send?

Step 1: Look for a point on the graph where the lines touch one another. Then follow that point down to the horizontal axis to see what time it was. At 7:00 P.M., they had each sent 40 messages.

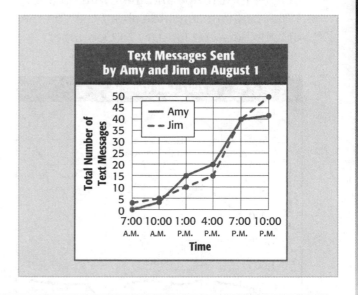

Text Messages Sent by Amy and Jim on August 1

Exercises   INTERPRET

1 What can you say about the supply and demand of chocolates from the double-line graph?

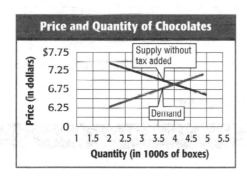

Price and Quantity of Chocolates

_____

_____

2 What conclusion can you draw from the double-line graph about grades and how much television is watched?

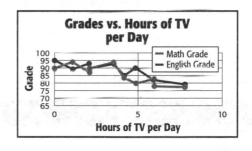

Grades vs. Hours of TV per Day

_____

_____

3 What conclusion can you draw about the temperatures in Hawaii and Wisconsin by looking at the double-line graph?

_____

_____

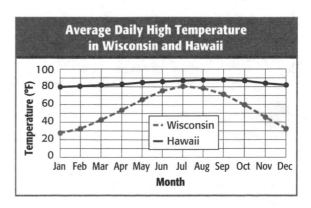

Average Daily High Temperature in Wisconsin and Hawaii

4 The graph displays the volume (number) of calls for Europe and the United States. What can you conclude about the volume of calls between January to December?

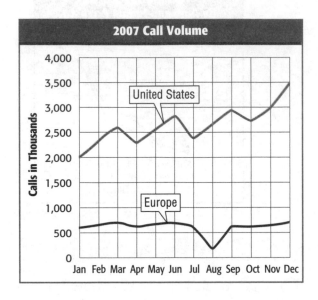

_____

_____

5 The double-line graph shows the amount of time that a single family house and a condominium stay on the market before they are sold. What conclusion can you make about the relationship?

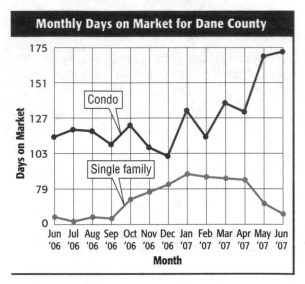

_____

_____

6 What can you determine about the sales figures for Harry and Kate?

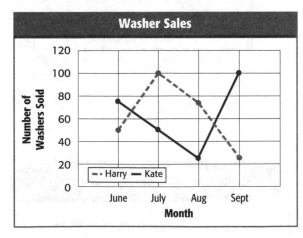

_____

_____

7 What can you conclude from the double-line graph about Lisa's Book Collection between January and May?

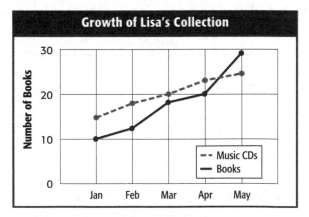

_____

_____

Circle Graphs

A **circle graph** compares parts of a whole to the whole. Some people refer to a circle graph as a pie chart, because it looks like a pie that is sliced up. When you read a circle graph, it does not always matter how big the whole is, because you are comparing parts to each other and to the whole. However, sometimes you can calculate a part exactly.

Examples:

Which kind of coin did Pat save the most?

Step 1: Find the biggest **segment** of the graph.

Step 2: Read the label for that segment. Pat saved more quarters than any other kind of coin.

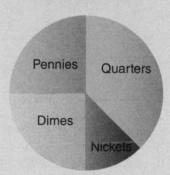

Coins in Pat's Bank

Pat saved a total of 64 coins. How many of them were pennies?

Step 1: Look at the whole circle. You may not be able to tell exactly how big each part is. However, you can estimate. If you compare pennies and dimes to the whole circle, those two **segments** account for half the circle.

Step 2: Multiply $\frac{1}{2} \times 64 = 32$. Altogether there are 32 pennies and dimes.

Step 3: Now compare the pennies and the dimes to each other. The segments look the same. So $\frac{1}{2}$ of those 32 coins are pennies and $\frac{1}{2}$ are dimes.

Step 4: Multiply $\frac{1}{2} \times 32 = 16$. There are 16 pennies.

Exercises · INTERPRET

1 In the circle graph, which is the smallest department in terms of new hires for the year?

_____

2 The circle graphs display how people in a company communicated in 2004 and 2008. What information can you gather from the two graphs?

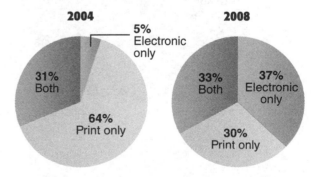

_____

3 Is the total of items A, E, and B more than C and D?

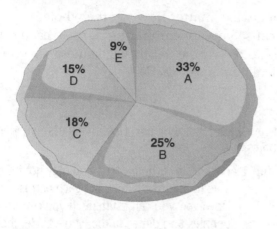

9%
E

15%
D

33%
A

18%
C

25%
B

_____

4 Do the Americas represent more than 50% of the total?

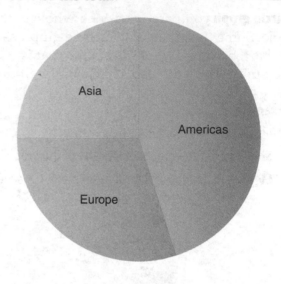

Asia

Americas

Europe

_____

5 According to the circle graph, are the combined sales for Atlanta and Sydney more than sales for Paris?

Total Sales by City

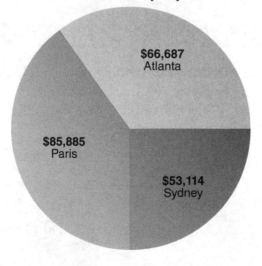

$66,687
Atlanta

$85,885
Paris

$53,114
Sydney

_____

6 In the circle graph, which age group makes up the majority of students who attend Basic Skills Summer School?

Basic Skills Summer School – Students by Age

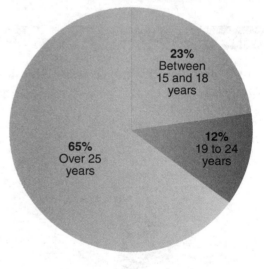

23%
Between
15 and 18
years

12%
19 to 24
years

65%
Over 25
years

_____

Measures of Central Tendency (Mean, Median, Range)

Statistics is a branch of math that studies data expressed in numbers. In the data, the numbers answer questions like: How many? How long? How far? How big?

Let's say you have this set of numbers: 21, 10, 18, 10, 14, 7, 10, 14

Begin by arranging them in order: 7, 10, 10, 10, 14, 14, 18, 21

The **range** is the greatest number minus the smallest number. $21 - 7 = 14$

> **Remember...**
> The range, mean, median, and mode numbers may all be different! Or some of them may be identical.

The **mean** (sometimes called the average) is the total of the whole collection divided by the number of addends. $104 \div 8 = 13$.

The **median** is the number in the middle. If your collection has an even number of addends, the median is the average of the two middle ones. $(10 + 14) \div 2 = 24 \div 2 = 12$

The **mode** is the number that appears most often in the collection. 10

> **Example:**
> Find the mean of 5, 3, 6, 10, 5, 2, 4
> **Step 1:** Add the numbers:
> $5 + 3 + 6 + 10 + 5 + 2 + 4 = 35$
> **Step 2:** Divide by the number of addends:
> $35 \div 7 = 5$

Exercises CALCULATE

1 What is the range for this set of numbers?
1, 8, 14, 22, 13, 19

_____

2 What is the average for this set of numbers?
2, 2, 3, 3, 4, 6, 6, 10

_____

3 What is the mode of this set of numbers?
2, 5, 10, 15, 6, 5, 6, 2, 5

_____

4 What is the median for this set of numbers?
3, 7, 2, 8, 9, 4, 6

_____

5 What is the range for this set of numbers?
2, 4, 9, 34, 35, 42, 15, 14

_____

6 What is the mean for this set of numbers?
10, 20, 30, 69, 79, 89, 3

_____

7 George earns tips of $10 for Sunday, $15 for Monday, and $35 for Tuesday. What is the average of his tips for the three days?

_____

8 If a group of 20 students in a class has an average age of 13 years, what would happen to the average if a student who was 12 years old was replaced with a student who was 14 years old?

_____

Name _____

Stem-and-Leaf Plots

A **stem-and-leaf plot** organizes data and helps
you compare it. Think of the plot as a plant
with stems. Each stem may have a different
number of leaves.

Example:

To read this, attach each leaf to its stem. In Mrs. Levy's
math class, the test scores were 66, 67, 68, 74, 75, 75,
82, 84, 86, 88, 88, 90, 90, 92, and 98. You will notice
that the data is organized from least to greatest.

In this stem-and-leaf plot, the stems are the scores (in
tens) and the leaves are the ones of the scores. To find
the **range** in a stem-and-leaf plot, look at the first leaf
on the first stem and the last leaf on the last stem.
Subtract the smaller number from the larger one.

Range = 98 − 66 = 32

Math Test Scores in Mrs. Smith's Math Class	
Stems	**Leaves**
6	6 7 8
7	4 5 5
8	2 4 6 8 8
9	0 0 2 8

Exercises   INTERPRET

1 What are the data points in this stem-and-
leaf plot? What is the range?

Stems	Leaves
1	9
2	2 5 6
3	0
4	
5	2 3 5
6	2

_____

_____

_____

Range: _____

2 Make a stem-and-leaf plot from the
following data:
55, 75, 77, 79, 82, 83, 84, 88, 89, 90, 95

Stems	Leaves

Name _____

Box-and-Whisker Plots

A **box-and-whisker plot** allows you to look at data to tell where most of the numbers lie. Thus, this type of plot shows the medians in the data.

Example:

You have recorded the heights, in inches, of the 13 children you baby-sit for. You arranged these numbers in order:
21, 23, 26, 30, 34, 34, 36, 36, 37, 38, 40, 48, 52

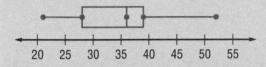

The **lower extreme** is the lowest number in your data. The **upper extreme** is the highest number in your data. The median of all the numbers in the data is the middle number, 36.

The **lower quartile** is the median of the numbers below the median.
$(26 + 30) \div 2 = 28$

The **upper quartile** is the median of the numbers above the median.
$(38 + 40) \div 2 = 39$

You have four sections on your line of data: each relates to its quartile mark, and each quartile mark relates to the median. Each quartile contains $\frac{1}{4}$ of the data.

What is the range of the lowest quartile?

Step 1: Find the lower extreme and the lower quartile. 21 and 28

Step 2: Subtract the lower extreme from the lower quartile. $28 - 21 = 7$

Exercises   SOLVE

1 What is the approximate median of the data in the box-and-whisker plot?

Weight

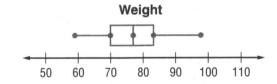

_____

2 The middle 50% of the data is between what two values?

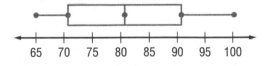

_____

3 What is the range of the data in the box-and-whisker plot?

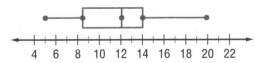

_____

4 What is the approximate range of the lowest 25% of the data in the box-and-whisker plot?

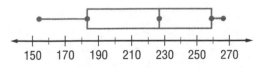

_____

5 What is the range of the top 75% of the scores in the box-and-whisker plot?

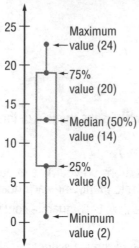

Range: _____

6 What is the range and median of the box-and-whisker plot?

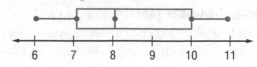

Range: _____

Median: _____

7 What is the approximate range of the third quartile?

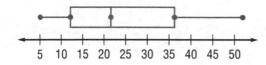

_____

8 What can you determine about the different quartiles in the box-and-whisker plot?

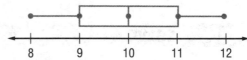

_____

9 What can you say about a student who weighs 155 lbs, if he is part of the group below?

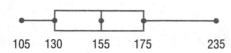

_____

10 What is the median of the box-and-whisker plot?

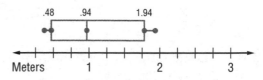

_____

Tree Diagrams

A **tree diagram** can be used to show possible combinations of people, places, or things. It looks like a set of trees with branches.

Example:

At a school cookout, you can buy a ticket that allows you to choose one main item, and one side dish. The tree diagram shows the possible combinations.

To find out how many possible combinations there are, count the number of branches. In this example there are nine branches.

How many possible combinations would there be if you could also order chips as a side?

Add chips as a branch on each item. Since there are 3 items, add $9 + 3 = 12$.

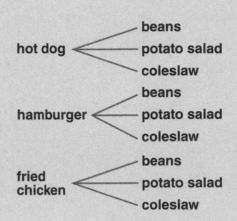

Exercises   INTERPRET

1 How many different outcomes are there in the tree diagram?

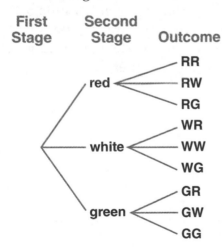

2 Below is a tree diagram of the choices at the picnic you are going to attend. If you do not like hamburgers, how many different meal combinations can you select from?

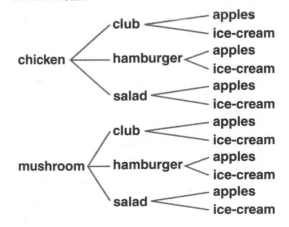

Name _____

Tree Diagrams (cont.)

Exercises   SOLVE

3 Draw a tree diagram that shows the possible outcomes of flipping a coin 3 times.

4 How many outcomes are there where both John and Bill fail?

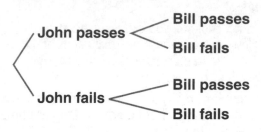

_____

_____

5 Below is a tree diagram of the possibilities where four girls—Heather, Alice, Lucy, and Annie—each choose one item for their desk. How many different outcomes are there where a pen is not chosen?

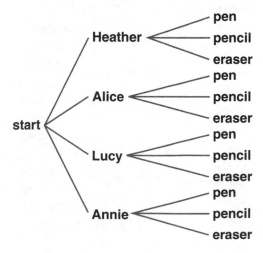

_____

_____

6 You are at an ice cream shop and you have three choices of ice cream—vanilla, strawberry, and chocolate. You have to choose a topping of either nuts or sprinkles. Draw a tree diagram that shows all the possible different ice cream cones you can order.

Venn Diagrams

A **Venn Diagram** is used to show groups of data and can show if and when some of the data can be placed in more than one group.

Example:

The left circle shows the days Sandra played only computer games. The right circle shows the days she played only soccer. The overlap area shows the days she played both games. Some data does not fit into the diagram at all. Using the data shown in this diagram, identify the day Sandra played none of the games identified in the data and tell why you choose that day. In this case, the day shown outside the diagram is the day Sandra played none of the listed games.

Games Played by Sandra in a Week

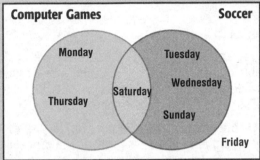

Exercises   INTERPRET

1 In a survey of 75 pet owners, 14 people owned pet birds and 31 owned tropical fish. The remaining people owned both a pet bird and tropical fish. What number should be placed in the intersecting area of the diagram?

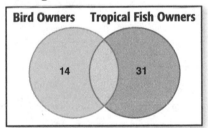

2 200 students at Edgewater Middle School were surveyed about their favorite type of music. Every student listened to either Hip Hop or Rock music. Some listened to both. Examine the Venn Diagram and calculate how many students listen only to Hip Hop.

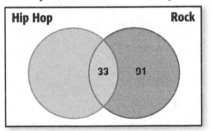

3 In a survey, 50 students filled out food preferences. What number should be be placed in the intersecting area?

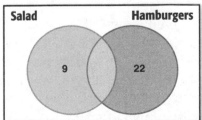

4 This Venn Diagram shows data about gum preferences. How many people participated in the survey?

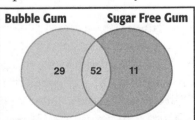

24.6

Calculating Probabilities

Probability is the likelihood of something happening in the future. Knowing how to calculate probability will help you predict future events, although not with 100 percent accuracy!

The simple formula to figure out probability (P) is the number of favorable outcomes (f) divided by the total number of possible outcomes (o). You could express this formula as an equation. $P = \frac{f}{o}$

Example:

If you roll one die of a pair of dice, there are six possible outcomes. Each die is a cube with six sides. Each side has a different number of spots. The die could show 1, 2, 3, 4, 5, or 6 spots.

What is the probability of the side with four spots being on top after the die is thrown? The probability of rolling a $4 = \frac{1}{6}$

What is the probability of a 5 or a 6 not being on top after a die is thrown?

Step 1: Decide how many favorable outcomes there are. $6 - 2 = 4$

Step 2: Set up your equation. $P = \frac{4}{6}$

Step 3: You could simplify that fraction. $\frac{4}{6} = \frac{2}{3}$

If you were to roll the die three times, you would probably have a favorable outcome two of those times.

Exercises   CALCULATE

1 If there are 20 boys in your class of 35 students, what is the probability that your teacher will call on a girl student?

_____

2 There are 12 green apples in the bag of 40 apples. What is the probability that you will get a green apple when you reach into the bag?

_____

3 You decide to watch a movie. There are 3 scary movies in a stack of 12 DVDs. What is the probability that you will pick a scary movie?

_____

4 John knows that once a week his mother makes steamed spinach. What is the probability that when John has dinner tonight that he will not have spinach?

_____

5 The department of motor vehicles noted that among passenger vehicles, there are 6 SUVs registered for every 12 cars registered in the state. What is the probability that the first vehicle you see on the street will be an SUV?

_____

6 In any given crowd of 20 people, 17 will be carrying cell phones, and 3 of those cell phones will have low batteries. What is the probability that when you ask a random person to borrow a cell phone, that you get one with a low battery?

_____

Unit Test

Lessons 23–24

1 Look at the chart of Walter's Dog House sales of hot dogs.

On what day were the most hot dogs sold? _____

The fewest? _____

About how many more hot dogs were sold on Sunday than Saturday? _____

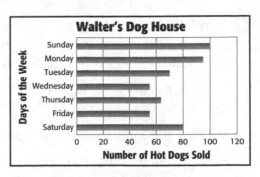

Walter's Dog House

2 Look at the line graph of school dance ticket sales. In what month were the most tickets sold? _____

About how many tickets were sold that month? _____

In what month were the fewest tickets sold? _____

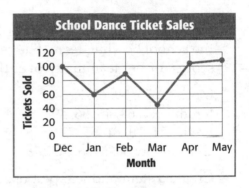

School Dance Ticket Sales

3 Look at the double-line graph of teenage employment rates. At which age are a higher percentage of British teenagers employed than Canadian teenagers? _____

Based on this line graph, would you say it is easier for a fourteen-year-old to find a job in Canada or Great Britain? _____

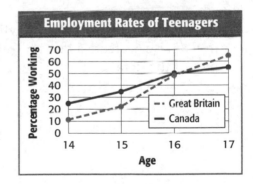

Employment Rates of Teenagers

4 Look at the circle graph of favorite breakfast foods. What is the favorite breakfast food as voted on by students? _____

Do more students prefer cereal than meat and eggs combined? _____

If so, by what percentage? _____

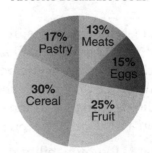

Favorite Breakfast Foods

Lessons 23–24

5 Bird Watchers of America was conducting its annual census for birds of prey. They recorded the following number of daily sightings for a ten-day period in October: 6, 8, 10, 10, 14, 9, 8, 10, 6, 5

What is the average number (mean) of sightings per day? _____

What is the median of the sample of daily sightings? _____

What is the mode of the sample of daily sightings? _____

6 Freda has been appointed the official scorekeeper for the school bowling team. She recorded the following scores for her teammates over the past two weeks:

Marissa: 55, 59, 63, 71, 45
Jeremy: 65, 64, 46, 56, 49
Freda: 71, 78, 81, 65, 72
Charmaine: 56, 59, 60, 65, 76

Create a stem-and-leaf plot using the data.

Stems	Leaves

7 Using the raw data for the bowling scores in Exercise 6, create a box-and-whisker plot of the data.

What is the range of the data? _____

What is the median of the data? _____

8 Eddie gathered stones from a nearby stream. He collected 12 stones in all and he noticed that 8 were black and 4 were white before he put them in a bag. Draw a tree diagram to show the possible outcomes if Eddie were to pick a stone from the bag, record the color, and return the stone to the bag and pick again.

What is the probability that Eddie will pick a black stone on the first pick? _____

What is the probability that Eddie will pick a white stone on the first pick? _____

Name _____

Lessons 23-24

9 Priscilla recorded the arrival of the members of her book club. She noted that there were 25 members in attendance. 16 brought dessert and 15 brought beverages. Draw a Venn Diagram and record the data.

How many in the book group brought dessert and beverages? _____

What percentage brought beverages only? _____

10 Wallace and 15 other students each put their names on a piece of paper and put them in a cap.

If there are 9 girls in the group, what is the probability that a girl's name will be picked from the cap? _____

What is the probability that Wallace's name will not be chosen? _____

11 Sue randomly throws darts at a wall covered with 100 balloons, 40 of which are red, 25 blue, 20 green, 10 yellow, and 5 orange.

What is the probability that Sue will pop a red or green balloon? _____

What is the probability that Sue will pop an orange balloon? _____

What is the probability that Sue will not pop a blue balloon? _____

Posttest

Complete the following test items.

1 There are three hundred thousand, two hundred, fifty two people living in Cincinnati. How would you write this number in standard form? _____

2 Jerry is collecting newspapers for a recycling contest at his school. He needs 2,152 newspapers to win the contest. So far he has collected 1,375. Rounding to the nearest thousand, how many newspapers can we estimate that Jerry still needs to collect? _____

Calculate.

3
$$\begin{array}{r} 27 \\ \times\ 17 \\ \hline \end{array}$$

4
$$\begin{array}{r} 9 \\ \times\ 56 \\ \hline \end{array}$$

5
$$\begin{array}{r} 72 \\ \times\ 81 \\ \hline \end{array}$$

6
$$\begin{array}{r} 32 \\ \times\ 28 \\ \hline \end{array}$$

7 Marcia bought 13 apple pies for her class, but her classmates only ate half of each pie. How would Marcia express the amount of remaining apple pie as an improper fraction? _____

Calculate.

8
$$\begin{array}{r} \$29.81 \\ \$14.33 \\ +\ \$31.11 \\ \hline \end{array}$$

9
$$\begin{array}{r} \$109.45 \\ -\ \$25.76 \\ \hline \end{array}$$

10
$$\begin{array}{r} \$3.43 \\ +\ \$7.07 \\ \hline \end{array}$$

11
$$\begin{array}{r} \$56.01 \\ +\ \$110.86 \\ \hline \end{array}$$

12 Ellen has been measuring the amount of snowfall for the last three months. She measured 1.262 inches in November, 1.794 inches in December, and 2.115 inches in January. Rounding to the nearest tenth of an inch, what was the total amount of snowfall during these three months? _____

Calculate.

13 $79\overline{)1591}$

14 $35\overline{)630}$

15 $15\overline{)78}$

16 $12\overline{)160}$

17 Marvin is mixing the paint he will use to paint his living room. The directions call for him to mix 23.75 milliliters of black paint and 9.20 milliliters of white paint to achieve the correct shade of grey. How much black paint and how much white paint will he need in order to apply four coats of paint? _____

About how much of the grey paint will he be making? _____

18 What is 40% of 150? _____

19 What is 20% of $\frac{4}{5}$? Express the number in both decimal and fraction form.

_____

20 Julia has a length of rope that is $17\frac{1}{4}$ meters long. If thirty percent of the rope's length has been painted blue, what length of the rope is not blue? _____

21 Put the following decimals in order from least to greatest:
.0245, .06, .0003, .75, .029, .9, .0019, 3.084, .0925, .21

_____

22 Rob bought a scale that records weight digitally. His small luggage bag weighs 10.279 kilograms, his laptop bag weighs 15.653 kilograms, his clothing bag weighs 25.455 kilograms, and his large bag weighs 35.350 kilograms. What is the total weight of the four bags, in kilograms?

_____

If a passenger is only allowed to carry 90 kilograms of luggage onto a flight, will Rob's luggage exceed the limit? _____

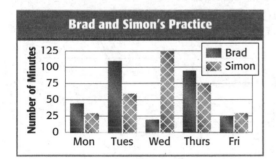

23 The chart shows how much time Brad and Simon spent practicing the clarinet last week. On which day did Brad practice for 95 minutes? _____

On which day did Simon practice 105 minutes longer than Brad? _____

24 Which city is colder in June? _____

During which month is the difference in temperature the greatest? _____

25 Frank is looking at a solid figure that has two circular ends. It also has curved sides. What shape is he looking at?

_____

Name _____

26 Tyler puts 5 nickels, 3 dimes, and 10 pennies into a hat. If you were to reach into that hat, what is the probability that you would pick a penny? _____ A dime? _____ A nickel? _____

27 Which of the following triangles is

obtuse? _____

right? _____

acute? _____

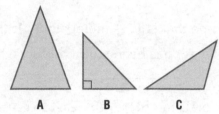

28 Calculate the following expression: $3 + (7 - 2)^2 + 4(5 + 3) - 6(6) =$ _____

29 Write the following number using scientific notation: 2,345,836.0071.

_____

30 Michael collects postcards and state flags. His collection consists of 3 postcards and 1 flag from New Hampshire, 5 postcards and 2 flags from Florida, and 7 postcards from Ohio. If each postcard costs $.50 and each flag costs $4.50, how much did Michael spend for his collection? _____

31 Which of the following angles is

acute? _____

right? _____

obtuse? _____

32 $28 \div .25 =$ _____   **33** $.3606 \div .06 =$ _____

34 What is $\frac{22}{31} \div 7$? _____   **35** What is $18 \div \frac{4}{15}$? _____   **36** What is $\frac{38}{51} \div \frac{19}{17}$? _____

Name _____

37 Latasha is in charge of providing bottled water and trail mix for her class field trip. Each student will be carrying $\frac{3}{5}$ liters of water and $\frac{1}{4}$ pound of trail mix during the trip. If there are 35 students on the trip, how much water and trail mix should Latasha bring for the class? _____

38 Last week Matthew spent $5\frac{1}{6}$ hours repairing his bike over a period of $3\frac{1}{3}$ days. How many hours a day, on average, did Matthew spend working on his bike? _____

39 What is the decimal form of $9\frac{3}{8}$? _____   **40** What is the fraction form of 3.6? _____

41 Daniel is making chocolate chip cookies for his classmates at school. Each batch requires $3\frac{2}{3}$ cups of sugar and $\frac{1}{3}$ of a bag of chocolate chips. If Daniel makes 4 batches of cookies, how many cups of sugar and how many bags of chocolate chips will he use? _____

42 What is $\frac{1}{3}$ of 72%? _____   **43** What is 60% of $\frac{1}{4}$

in decimal form? _____

in fraction form? _____

44 What is the perimeter and area of the figure?

Perimeter _____

Area _____

5 cm

7 cm

45 One inch is equivalent to 2.54 centimeters.
How many inches is 4 meters?
How many centimeters are in 254 inches?

_____ inches = 4 meters   254 inches = _____ centimeters

Glossary

Addend: Any number that is added to another number. *(p. 73)*

Acute Angle: An angle with a measure of less than 90°. *(p. 106)*

Acute Triangle: A triangle with only acute angles, angles less than 90°. *(p. 109)*

Algebra: A branch of math used to find the value of unknown variables. *(p. 76)*

Algebraic Expression: A group of letters, numbers, and symbols used in a series of operations. *(p. 75)*

Angle: Two rays that share an endpoint. *(p. 106)*

Area: The measure of a 2- or 3-dimensional figure's interior, given in square units. *(p. 90)*

Associative Property of Addition: States that addends may be grouped in any order without changing the sum. *(p. 73)*

Associative Property of Multiplication: States that numbers may be grouped in any way without changing the product. *(p. 73)*

Bar Graph: A graph that uses numbers to compare two or more people, places, or things. Each bar represents a number and may be represented horizontally or vertically. *(p. 119)*

Base: The face on the bottom of a solid figure. *(p. 114)*

Base of an Exponent: The number being used as the factor when writing in exponential form. In the statement 10^3, the base is 10. *(p. 70)*

Box-and-Whisker Plot: Organizes data to show where the most data points lie and also shows the median of the data. *(p. 129)*

Carry: To place an extra digit—when adding or multiplying—in the next place-value column on the left. *(p. 10)*

Celsius: Used in the metric system to measure temperature and expressed as °C, also expressed as Centigrade. *(p. 93)*

Chord: A line segment with both endpoints on a circle's circumference. *(p. 112)*

Circle: A 2-dimensional figure with every point on its circumference an equal distance from its center point. *(p. 112)*

Circle Graph: Shows parts of a whole as a percentage to the whole and is also known as a pie chart. *(p. 125)*

Circumference: The length of distance around a circle's perimeter. *(p. 112)*

Coefficient: The number that replaces the symbol × and multiplies the variable in a multiplication expression. The statement $9m$ shows 9 as the coefficient and m as the variable. *(p. 76)*

Common Denominator: A number which can be divided evenly by all the denominators in a group of fractions. *(p. 26)*

Common Multiple: A number that can be divided evenly by two or more different numbers. *(p. 26)*

Commutative Property of Additions: States that numbers may be added in any order without changing the sum. *(p. 73)*

Commutative Property of Multiplication: States that multiplication may be done in any order without changing the product. *(p. 73)*

Compatible Numbers: Numbers that are easy to work with in your head. *(p. 18)*

Complementary Angles: Two angles that form a right angle. Their sum is 90°. *(p. 107)*

Congruent: A term used to describe polygons whose shape and size are the same. *(p. 111)*

Cross-multiplying: A method for finding a missing numerator or denominator. *(p. 39)*

Customary Units of Length: Measurements expressed in inches (in.), feet (ft), yards (yd), and miles (mi). *(p. 86)*

Customary Units of Liquid Volume: Measurements expressed in cups (c), pints (pt), quarts (qt), and gallons (gal). *(p. 87)*

Customary Units of Weight: Measurements expressed in ounces (oz), pounds (lb), and tons. *(p. 88)*

Denominator: The number below the line in a fraction. *(p. 22)*

Diameter: A chord that passes through a circle's center point. *(p. 112)*

Distributive Property of Multiplication: States that each number may be multiplied separately and added together for the product. *(p. 74)*

Dividend: The number to be divided in a division problem. *(p. 16)*

Divisor: The number by which another number—the dividend—will be divided. *(p. 16)*

Double-Line Graph: Compares how information changes as time passes between two or more people, places, or things. *(p. 123)*

Edge: The line on a solid figure where two faces meet. *(p. 114)*

Equality Property of Addition: States that when adding a number on one side of an equation, you must add the *same* number on the other side of an equation. Both sides will then still be equal. *(p. 75)*

Equality Property of Division: States that when dividing a number on one side of an equation, you must divide by the *same* number on the other side of the equation. Both sides will then still be equal. *(p. 75)*

Equality Property of Multiplication: States that when multiplying a number on one side of an equation, you must multiply by the *same* number on the other side of the equation. Both sides will then still be equal. *(p. 75)*

Equality Property of Subtraction: States that when subtracting a number on one side of an equation, you must subtract the *same* number on the other side of the equation. Both sides will then still be equal. *(p. 75)*

Equation: A mathematical statement used to show that two amounts are equal. *(p. 70)*

Equilateral Triangle: A triangle with all three sides being the same length. *(p. 109)*

Exponent: The number that tells how many times the base number is multiplied by itself. The exponent 3 in 10^3 shows $10 \times 10 \times 10$. *(p. 70)*

Exponential Expression: A base number and an exponent. 4^3 is an example of an exponential expression. *(p. 70)*

Face: The flat surface of a solid figure. On a solid figure each face looks two-dimensional. *(p. 114)*

Factors: Numbers that are multiplied. *(p. 54)*

Fahrenheit: The customary system used to measure temperature and expressed as °F. *(p. 93)*

Fluid Ounces: A measurement of liquid volume. *(p. 99)*

Gram: The basic metric unit of mass, expressed as (g). *(p. 96)*

Grid: A device with a horizontal axis and a vertical axis used to express the location of a point. *(p. 81)*

Identity Elements: Numbers in a problem that do not affect the answer. Only addition and multiplication have identity elements. *(p. 74)*

Improper Fraction: A fraction greater than 1 because its numerator is greater than its denominator. *(p. 22)*

Intersecting Lines: Lines that meet or cross each other at a specific point. *(p. 104)*

Interval: The distance between each measurement of time on a line graph. *(p. 121)*

Inverse: A number's exact opposite on the other side of the number line. The inverse of −9 is 9. *(p. 79)*

Isosceles Triangle: A triangle with two sides the same length but the third side being of a different length. *(p. 109)*

Kite: A quadrilateral with two angles that are equal, two touching sides that are equal in length, and the other two touching sides are equal in length. *(p. 110)*

Like Denominators: Fractions that have the same denominator. (p. 24)

Line: A straight path that goes in both directions and does not end. A line is measured in length. (p. 104)

Line Graph: Often used to show a change in information as time passes. The distance from one time to another is an interval. (p. 121)

Line Segment: A specific part of a line that ends at two identified points. (p. 105)

Liquid Volume: Measures the amount of liquid a container can hold and expressed in cups (c), pints (pt), quarts (qt), and gallons (gal). (p. 87)

Liter: The basic metric unit of liquid volume, expressed as (L). There are also milliliters (mL), centiliters (cL), and kiloliters (kL). (p. 95)

Lower Extreme: The lowest number in a group of numbers used in a box-and-whisker plot. (p. 129)

Lower Quartile: The median of numbers from the lower extreme to the median on a box-and-whisker plot. (p. 129)

Mean: The total number of the whole collection divided by the number of addends. In the expression $104 \div 8 = 13$, 13 is the mean. (p. 127)

Median: The middle number in a set of numbers when the numbers are arranged from least to greatest. (p. 127)

Metric Units of Length: Measurements expressed in millimeters (mm), centimeters (cm), meters (m), and kilometers (km). (p. 94)

Metric Units of Liquid Volume: Measurements expressed in liter (L), milliliters (mL), centiliters (cL), and kiloliters (kL). (p. 95)

Metric Units of Mass: Measurements expressed in grams (g), milligrams (mg), centigrams (cg), and kilograms (kg). (p. 96)

Mixed Number: A number with a whole number part and a fraction part. (p. 22)

Mode: The number that appears most often in a set of numbers. (p. 127)

Negative Number: A number less than 0 and identified with the minus sign. (p. 79)

Numerator: The number above the line in a fraction. (p. 22)

Obtuse Angle: An angle with a measure of more than $90°$. (p. 106)

Obtuse Triangle: A triangle with one obtuse angle. (p. 109)

Ordered Pair: Numbers used to identify a point on a grid. (p. 81)

Order of Operations: Rules that tell the steps to follow when doing a computation. (p. 72)

Origin: The point on a grid where the vertical and horizontal axes meet. (p. 81)

Percent: A special ratio that compares a number to 100 using the % symbol. (p. 63)

Perimeter: The distance around a figure. (p. 89)

Pi: The ratio of a circle's diameter to its circumference—a ratio that is exactly the same for every circle. A circle's circumference equals pi times its diameter. A circle's area equals pi times the square of its radius. Pi is often rounded to 3.14. (p. 113)

Place Value: The value of a position of a digit in a number. (p. 8)

Point: An exact location in space that has no dimensions and cannot be measured. A point is usually represented by a dot. (p. 104)

Polygon: Any closed two-dimensional figure that is made up of line segments. Triangles and quadrilaterals are two types of polygons. (p. 111)

Probability: The likelihood of an event happening in the future. (p. 133)

Product: The result, or answer, of a multiplication problem. (p. 13)

Property of Additive Inverse: States that when adding a negative number to its inverse, the sum will be 0. For example: $-8 + 8 = 0$. (p. 79)

Proportion: A problem that contains two ratios that are equal. (p. 39)

Quadrilateral: A two-dimensional figure with four sides and four angles. (p. 110)

Quotient: The result of dividing one number by another. (p. 16)

Radius: A line segment that starts at a circle's center point and extends to its perimeter. (p. 112)

Range: The greatest number minus the smallest number in a set of numbers. (p. 127)

Ratio: A comparison of two numbers using division. (p. 138)

Ray: A part of a line that extends from a specific point in only one direction. (p. 105)

Reciprocals: Two fractions that look like upside-down reflections of one another. (p. 31)

Regrouping: In place value, to use part of the value from one place in another place to make adding or subtracting easier. (p. 10)

Remainder: The number left over in whole-number division when you can no longer divide any further. (p. 16)

Rhombus: A quadrilateral where both pairs of sides are parallel and have the same length. All angles are less than $90°$. (p. 110)

Right Angle: An angle that measures exactly $90°$. (p. 106)

Right Triangle: A triangle with one right angle. (p. 109)

Rounding: To drop or zero-out digits in a number to a higher or lower value. (p. 12)

Scalene Triangle: A triangle with all three sides being of different lengths. (p. 109)

Solid Figure: A *three*-dimensional figure such as a cube or pyramid. (p. 114)

Statistics: A branch of math that answers questions about how many, how long, how often, how far, or how big. (p. 127)

Stem-and-Leaf Plot: Used to organize data and compare it. A stem-and-leaf plot organizes data from least to greatest using the digits or the greatest place value to group data. (p. 128)

Supplementary Angles: Any two angles that add up to a sum of $180°$. (p. 107)

Tree Diagram: Used to show possible combinations of data including people, places, or things in a diagram that looks like a tree with branches. (p. 130)

Trapezoid: A quadrilateral that has two lines that are parallel to each other and two lines that are not parallel. (p. 110)

Triangle: A two-dimensional figure with three sides. (p. 109)

Upper Extreme: The highest number in a group of numbers used in a box-and-whisker plot. (p. 129)

Upper Quartile: The median of numbers from the median to the upper extreme in a box-and-whisker plot. (p. 129)

Variable: An unknown number usually expressed as a letter and used in Algebra. In the statement $n - 18$, n is the variable. (p. 76)

Venn Diagram: A diagram used to show data and how different sets of data can overlap. (p. 132)

Vertex: The specific point of a ray, also called an endpoint. (p. 105)

Vertex of a Solid: A specific point at which more than 2 faces meet, or a point where a curve begins. (p. 114)

Vertical Angles: The angles opposite each other when two lines intersect. (p. 107)

Volume: The number of units a solid figure contains, expressed in cubic inches, feet, or yards. (p. 91)

Whole Number: A number that does not include a fraction or decimal. (p. 10)

Zero Property of Multiplication: States that any number times zero equals zero. (p. 75)

Answers

Lesson 1.1

1. One thousands
2. Tenths
3. 5
4. 4
5. Ten millions
6. Six million seven hundred eighty-two thousand one hundred twenty-one
7. Hundredths
8. Hundreds
9. 9
10. Hundreds
11. $(3 \times 100,000) + (3 \times 1,000) + (2 \times 100) + (1 \times 1) + (3 \times .1) + (2 \times .01) + (1 \times .001)$
    Three hundred three thousand, two hundred one, and three hundred twenty-one thousandths
12. 732,998.207
    Seven hundred thirty-two thousand, nine hundred ninety-eight and two hundred seven thousandths
13. 12,454,721.096
    $(1 \times 10,000,000) + (2 \times 1,000,000) + (4 \times 100,000) + (5 \times 10,000) + (4 \times 1,000) + (7 \times 100) + (2 \times 10) + (1 \times 1) + (9 \times .01) + (6 \times .001)$
14. 4,063,500.207
    Four million, sixty-three thousand, five hundred and two hundred seven thousandths
    $(1 \times 1,000,000) + (5 \times 100,000) + (5 \times 10,000) + (9 \times 1,000) + (4 \times 100) + (6 \times 10) + (1 \times 1) + (6 \times .1) + (2 \times .01) + (5 \times .001)$
    One million, five hundred fifty-nine thousand, four hundred sixty-one and six hundred twenty-five thousandths

15. 444,236.056
    $(4 \times 100,000) + (4 \times 10,000) + (4 \times 1,000) + (2 \times 100) + (3 \times 10) + (6 \times 1) + (5 \times .01) + (6 \times .001)$
16. One thousand three hundred ninety-six

Lesson 1.2

Add

1. 11,446
2. 7,243
3. 103
4. 4,870
5. 3,558
6. 2,449
7. 660
8. 28,868
9. 4,492
10. 10,008
11. 646
12. 3,700
13. 1,889
14. 1,332
15. 589
16. 1,514
17. 858
18. 421
19. 610
20. 172

Subtract

1. 15
2. 27
3. 15
4. 98
5. 1,109
6. 1,002
7. 5,098
8. 1,112
9. 86
10. 138
11. 17
12. 2,787
13. 2,779
14. 91
15. 97

16. 898
17. 13
18. 2,876
19. 180
20. 82

Lesson 1.3

1. 70
2. 400
3. 40
4. 40
5. 90
6. 1,400
7. 40
8. 500
9. 100
10. 1,300
11. 1,300
12. 1,100
13. 6,000
14. 60,000
15. 200
16. 1,000
17. 4,000
18. 10,000
19. 10,000
20. 400

Lesson 2.1

1. 132
2. 240
3. 228
4. 154
5. 612
6. 1,395
7. 4,725
8. 26,220
9. 629,706
10. 972
11. 336
12. 101,244
13. 11,655
14. 462
15. 4,640
16. 3,190
17. 540

18. 4,488
19. 9,213
20. 205,270
21. 8,124
22. 17,280
23. 1,804
24. 50,765
25. 1,260
26. 19,642
27. 651
28. 1,804
29. 750 apples
30. 1600 baseball cards

Lesson 2.2

1. 400
2. 8,100
3. 100
4. 350,000
5. 10,000
6. 180,000
7. 2,100
8. 20,000
9. 1,500,000
10. 32,000
11. 3,600
12. 80,000
13. 35,000,000
14. 14,000
15. 20
16. 720,000
17. 6,000
18. 18,000
19. 450,000
20. 6,000,000

Lesson 3.1

1. 7 R4
2. 24 R5
3. 23 R1
4. 78 R6
5. 15 R2
6. 9 R3
7. 78 R11
8. 1,234 R8
9. 456 R2

10. 423 R5

11. 729 R2

12. 17 R5

13. 147 R6

14. 85 R6

15. 18 R5

16. 65 R1

17. 89 R2

18. 45 R4

19. 555 R2

20. 12 R1

21. 13 R1

22. 563 R3

23. 278 R3

24. 89 R4

25. 86 R3

26. 712 R12

27. 85 R5

28. 56 R4

29. 4 days

30. 18 new students

Lesson 3.2

1. 12

2. 30

3. 10

4. 30

5. 16

6. 100

7. 50

8. 20

9. 5

10. 10

11. 12

12. 40

13. 25

14. 20

15. 50

16. 12

17. 20

18. 20

19. 15

20. 80

Lesson 4.1

1. $3\frac{1}{7}$

2. $8\frac{3}{4}$

3. $7\frac{3}{10}$

4. $15\frac{2}{3}$

5. $7\frac{10}{11}$

6. $5\frac{5}{6}$

7. $5\frac{1}{5}$

8. $13\frac{7}{8}$

9. $10\frac{2}{3}$

10. $13\frac{1}{5}$

11. $19\frac{2}{11}$

12. $5\frac{1}{4}$

13. $11\frac{1}{7}$

14. $9\frac{1}{9}$

15. $6\frac{1}{2}$

16. $16\frac{3}{4}$

17. $1\frac{3}{8}$

18. $3\frac{1}{14}$

19. $10\frac{7}{13}$

20. $22\frac{1}{2}$

Lesson 4.2

1. $\frac{8}{3}$

2. $\frac{39}{7}$

3. $\frac{108}{5}$

4. $\frac{43}{8}$

5. $\frac{160}{7}$

6. $\frac{169}{11}$

7. $\frac{41}{3}$

8. $\frac{62}{17}$

9. $\frac{42}{19}$

10. $\frac{27}{4}$

11. $\frac{52}{51}$

12. $\frac{111}{2}$

13. $\frac{232}{23}$

14. $\frac{46}{7}$

15. $\frac{93}{7}$

16. $\frac{127}{3}$

17. $\frac{96}{19}$

18. $\frac{38}{3}$

19. $\frac{11}{4}$

20. $\frac{20033}{100}$

Lesson 4.3

1. 2

2. $\frac{13}{3}$

3. $\frac{12}{11}$

4. $\frac{7}{19}$

5. $\frac{9}{7}$

6. 2

7. 1

8. $\frac{26}{33}$

9. $\frac{8}{10}$ or $\frac{4}{5}$

10. $\frac{36}{37}$

11. $\frac{48}{97}$

12. $\frac{17}{23}$

13. $\frac{17}{13}$

14. $\frac{7}{9}$

15. $\frac{33}{39}$ or $\frac{11}{13}$

16. 1

17. $\frac{8}{14}$ or $\frac{4}{7}$

18. $\frac{13}{7}$

Lesson 4.4

1. $\frac{3}{7}$

2. $\frac{4}{13}$

3. $\frac{1}{11}$

4. $\frac{5}{21}$

5. $\frac{1}{3}$

6. 0

7. $\frac{25}{96}$

8. $\frac{1}{13}$

9. $\frac{15}{49}$

10. $\frac{20}{31}$

11. $\frac{3}{7}$

12. $\frac{3}{17}$

13. $\frac{1}{4}$

14. $\frac{10}{15}$ or $\frac{2}{3}$

15. $\frac{2}{12}$ or $\frac{1}{6}$

16. $\frac{4}{7}$

17. $\frac{2}{8}$ or $\frac{1}{4}$

18. $\frac{3}{13}$

Lesson 4.5

1. $\frac{31}{35}$

2. $\frac{38}{39}$

3. $\frac{7}{8}$

4. $\frac{43}{77}$

5. $\frac{23}{20}$

6. $\frac{15}{28}$

7. $\frac{5}{12}$

8. $\frac{17}{24}$

9. $\frac{121}{105}$

10. $\frac{10}{39}$

11. $\frac{19}{20}$

12. $\frac{7}{20}$

13. $\frac{25}{28}$

14. $\frac{1}{12}$

15. $\frac{28}{110}$ or $\frac{14}{55}$

16. $\frac{11}{16}$

Lesson 4.6

1. $4\frac{13}{15}$

2. $7\frac{26}{35}$

3. $7\frac{34}{63}$

4. $5\frac{35}{48}$

5. $12\frac{54}{77}$

6. $8\frac{17}{36}$

7. $23\frac{37}{56}$

8. $13\frac{27}{30}$

9. $16\frac{32}{63}$

10. $24\frac{17}{18}$

11. $5\frac{1}{15}$

12. $8\frac{1}{30}$

13. $6\frac{11}{36}$

14. $9\frac{11}{18}$

15. $7\frac{7}{72}$

16. $5\frac{11}{14}$

Answers

Lesson 4.7

1. $1\frac{3}{8}$

2. $2\frac{3}{28}$

3. $3\frac{1}{9}$

4. $2\frac{27}{40}$

5. $1\frac{1}{110}$

6. $1\frac{1}{12}$

7. $5\frac{19}{36}$

8. $3\frac{11}{42}$

9. $3\frac{5}{52}$

10. $16\frac{39}{70}$

11. $3\frac{13}{24}$

12. $3\frac{13}{90}$

13. $4\frac{5}{8}$ gallons

14. Yes, because she will have $1\frac{5}{8}$ pounds left

Lesson 4.8

1. 2

2. 1

3. 1

4. $1\frac{1}{2}$

5. 4

6. $12\frac{1}{2}$

7. $2\frac{1}{2}$

8. $6\frac{1}{2}$

9. $12\frac{1}{2}$

10. 9

11. $1\frac{1}{2}$

12. 3

13. About $21\frac{1}{2}$ ounces

14. About $4\frac{1}{2}$ cords

Lesson 5.1

1. $3\frac{3}{4}$ or $\frac{15}{4}$

2. $1\frac{1}{7}$ or $\frac{8}{7}$

3. $13\frac{1}{8}$ or $\frac{105}{8}$

4. $2\frac{4}{9}$ or $\frac{22}{9}$

5. $1\frac{1}{11}$ or $\frac{12}{11}$

6. $12\frac{1}{14}$ or $\frac{169}{14}$

7. $9\frac{3}{23}$ or $\frac{210}{23}$

8. $4\frac{2}{3}$ or $\frac{14}{3}$

9. $4\frac{8}{19}$ or $\frac{84}{19}$

10. $8\frac{2}{5}$ or $\frac{42}{5}$

11. $51\frac{1}{3}$ or $\frac{154}{3}$

12. $3\frac{1}{17}$ or $\frac{52}{17}$

13. $3\frac{21}{23}$ or $\frac{90}{23}$

14. $12\frac{9}{22}$ or $\frac{273}{22}$

15. $2\frac{16}{27}$ or $\frac{70}{27}$

16. $37.63

17. $6\frac{4}{5}$ miles

Lesson 5.2

1. $\frac{1}{4}$

2. $\frac{4}{7}$

3. $\frac{5}{33}$

4. $\frac{10}{39}$

5. 1

6. $\frac{7}{11}$

7. $\frac{7}{10}$

8. 1

9. $\frac{85}{81}$ or $1\frac{4}{81}$

10. $\frac{18}{55}$

11. $\frac{13}{21}$

12. $\frac{16}{25}$

13. 1

14. $\frac{40}{133}$

15. $\frac{99}{182}$

16. $\frac{16}{33}$

17. $\frac{1}{35}$

18. $\frac{25}{54}$

19. $\frac{11}{17}$

20. 1

Lesson 5.3

1. $1\frac{1}{5}$

2. $\frac{17}{18}$

3. $1\frac{17}{28}$

4. $2\frac{2}{3}$

5. $2\frac{38}{45}$

6. $\frac{10}{21}$

7. $3\frac{1}{2}$

8. $1\frac{25}{32}$

9. $1\frac{1}{3}$

10. $2\frac{10}{49}$

11. $1\frac{8}{9}$

12. 1

13. 4

14. $1\frac{11}{28}$

15. $4\frac{22}{23}$

Lesson 5.3 (cont.)

1. $3\frac{1}{3}$

2. $11\frac{11}{20}$

3. $13\frac{2}{3}$

4. $6\frac{19}{28}$

5. $2\frac{6}{7}$

6. $9\frac{1}{6}$

7. $5\frac{5}{9}$

8. $5\frac{7}{10}$

9. $7\frac{1}{2}$

10. $10\frac{11}{15}$

11. 15

12. $11\frac{11}{16}$

13. $1\frac{11}{16}$

14. $8\frac{9}{20}$

15. $10\frac{5}{16}$

Lesson 6.1

1. $\frac{1}{8}$

2. $\frac{3}{20}$

3. $\frac{6}{21}$ or $\frac{2}{7}$

4. $\frac{1}{12}$

5. $\frac{5}{38}$

6. $\frac{4}{35}$

7. $\frac{1}{81}$

8. $\frac{3}{132}$ or $\frac{1}{44}$

9. $\frac{17}{72}$

10. $\frac{12}{39}$ or $\frac{4}{13}$

11. $\frac{2}{18}$ or $\frac{1}{9}$

12. $\frac{5}{220}$ or $\frac{1}{44}$

13. $\frac{3}{77}$

14. $\frac{1}{27}$

15. $\frac{10}{55}$ or $\frac{2}{11}$

16. $\frac{10}{39}$

17. $\frac{4}{20}$ or $\frac{1}{5}$

18. $\frac{12}{65}$

19. $\frac{2}{44}$ or $\frac{1}{22}$

20. $\frac{3}{28}$

21. $\frac{1}{19}$ of a pound of chocolate each

22. $\frac{10}{39}$ liters of apple cider each

Lesson 6.2

1. 20

2. $\frac{15}{4}$ or $3\frac{3}{4}$

3. 49

4. $\frac{63}{4}$ or $15\frac{3}{4}$

5. 4

6. 14

7. 21

8. 18

9. $\frac{51}{2}$ or $25\frac{1}{2}$

10. $\frac{25}{3}$ or $8\frac{1}{3}$

11. 9

12. 6

13. 55

14. 4

15. 27

16. $\frac{6}{7}$

17. $\frac{55}{3}$ or $18\frac{1}{3}$

18. $\frac{3}{2}$ or $1\frac{1}{2}$

19. 78

20. 147

21. 68

22. 76

23. 9

24. 50

25. $\frac{51}{2}$ or $25\frac{1}{2}$

Answers

Lesson 6.3

1. $\frac{20}{21}$
2. $\frac{7}{3}$
3. $\frac{7}{27}$
4. $\frac{27}{4}$
5. $\frac{27}{26}$
6. $\frac{1}{3}$
7. $\frac{10}{13}$
8. $\frac{3}{2}$
9. $\frac{16}{3}$
10. $\frac{45}{16}$
11. 6
12. $\frac{3}{4}$
13. $\frac{3}{242}$
14. 9
15. $\frac{5}{2}$

Lesson 6.4

1. $\frac{3}{5}$
2. $\frac{16}{5}$ or $3\frac{1}{5}$
3. $\frac{15}{7}$ or $2\frac{1}{7}$
4. $\frac{125}{84}$ or $1\frac{41}{84}$
5. 2
6. $\frac{22}{15}$ or $1\frac{7}{15}$
7. $\frac{19}{11}$ or $1\frac{8}{11}$
8. $\frac{26}{7}$ or $3\frac{5}{7}$
9. 3 batches of cookies
10. 14 balloons

Lesson 7.1

1. $2.14 or $\frac{15}{7}$ dollars
2. 65 miles per day
3. $16\frac{2}{3}$ quarts per cylinder
4. $\frac{1}{5}$ pound of butter per loaf
5. 25 tons per mile
6. 4 slices of pizza per person
7. $\frac{1}{5}$ needs to be painted
8. $\frac{8}{23}$ filled

Lesson 7.2

1. $x = 16$
2. $x = 20$
3. $x = 17$
4. $x = 14$
5. $x = 4$
6. $x = 2$
7. $x = 4$
8. $x = 17$
9. $x = 78$
10. $x = 2$
11. $x = 55$
12. $x = 16$
13. $x = 104$
14. $x = 341$
15. $x = 12$
16. $x = 3$
17. $x = 20$
18. $x = 484$
19. $x = 10$
20. $x = 27$
21. $x = 2,662$
22. $x = 63$
23. $x = 16$
24. $x = 12$
25. $x = 42$
26. $x = 12$
27. $x = 164$
28. $x = 7$

Lesson 7.3

1. 17 days
2. 168 km
3. 10 miles
4. 4 hours
5. 84 acres
6. $2\frac{1}{2}$ minutes
7. 840 square feet
8. 105 minutes

Lesson 7.4

1. About 135 miles
2. 210 acres
3. 55 minutes
4. 78 pizzas
5. $94.29
6. 9 workers
7. 1248 bushels
8. 495 pounds

Lesson 8.1

1. 68
2. 18
3. 22
4. 48
5. 76
6. 18.5
7. 21.2
8. 44.4
9. 11.1
10. 59.5
11. 429.35
12. 39.75
13. 313.31
14. 528.46
15. 832.83
16. 32.346
17. 1.414
18. 12.173
19. 592.422
20. 837.820

Lesson 8.2

1. .25
2. .875
3. .1111
4. .7143
5. .4545
6. .3684
7. .1923
8. .9773
9. .1304
10. .5333

Lesson 8.3

1. $\frac{9}{20}$
2. $\frac{47}{100}$
3. $\frac{7}{5}$
4. $\frac{17}{25}$
5. $\frac{11}{50}$
6. $\frac{1}{4}$
7. $\frac{15}{4}$
8. $\frac{13}{16}$
9. $\frac{15}{8}$
10. $\frac{11}{100}$
11. $\frac{4}{5}$
12. $\frac{1}{8}$
13. $\frac{13}{20}$
14. $\frac{53}{100}$
15. $\frac{11}{25}$
16. 11 measuring cups of flour and 1 measuring cup of corn starch
17. $\frac{9}{10}$ miles

Lesson 8.4

1. .33, .333, .3333
2. .388, .39, .393, 1.39
3. .44, 4.439, 4.44, 4.441
4. 7.7777, 7.7778, 7.778, 7.78
5. .445, 4.45, 44.5, 445
6. 22.23222, 22.2323, 22.2332, 22.3
7. 1.765, 1.7655, 1.76559, 1.766
8. .08888, .09, .090001, 1.09
9. 9.98989, 9.998989, 9.999888, 9.9999888

Lesson 9.1

1. 3.685
2. 11.105
3. 1.353
4. 137.78
5. 48.6666
6. 53.4451
7. 2.761
8. 11.091
9. 22.211
10. 144.423
11. 345.345
12. 262.994
13. 578.0775
14. 101.651
15. 36.8155 feet
16. 33.547 seconds

Answers

Lesson 9.2

1. .02
2. 67.855
3. 20.12
4. 9.5
5. 12.018
6. .156
7. 20.994
8. 181.08
9. 1.856
10. 8.559
11. 291.662
12. 48.82
13. .4
14. 683.29
15. 1.48
16. 11.02

Lesson 9.3

1. $10.67
2. $137.01
3. $32.52
4. $6.45
5. $2.89
6. $6.85
7. $5.11
8. $54.78
9. $33.55
10. $98.00
11. $8.62
12. $107.96
13. $687.20
14. $9.77
15. $1.95
16. $12.98
17. $0.32
18. $18.02
19. $21.00
20. $2.87

Lesson 9.4

1. 51
2. 60
3. 67
4. 10
5. 6
6. $19.50
7. 1
8. $10.50
9. 47
10. $6.00
11. 90
12. 9

Lesson 10.1

1. 9,586.5
2. 54.39
3. 17,526.24
4. 110.11
5. 137,101.44
6. 20,340.9
7. 4,474.4
8. 1,747.2
9. 481.8
10. 1,484.7
11. 10.201
12. 308.025
13. 180.810
14. 145.2482
15. 1,730.3616
16. 8.37
17. 735.279
18. 3.83194
19. 553.125
20. 600.7002
21. 1,990
22. 24
23. .11234
24. .0156
25. 71,782
26. 76,760
27. 13.2
28. 63,450
29. .001345
30. 11.11111

Lesson 10.2

1. $26.13
2. $112.10
3. $21.60
4. $782.69
5. $40.10
6. $267.63
7. $455.63
8. $23.00
9. $60.50
10. $45.13
11. $426.50
12. $72.60
13. $24.71
14. Yes, he will. It will cost him $4.80 to buy 120 marbles.

Lesson 10.3

1. 160
2. $35
3. 500
4. 600
5. $100
6. 1
7. $55
8. 900
9. 30
10. $20
11. 25
12. 80
13. 250
14. $300
15. 4
16. $120
17. 70
18. 32
19. 20
20. $40

Lesson 11.1

1. 5.05
2. 5.6125
3. 7.825
4. 2.02
5. .96875
6. 2.9
7. 3.89
8. 1.515
9. 17.333
10. 27.9375
11. 25.39
12. 132.8
13. 278.15625
14. 4.02
15. 1.71875
16. 106.03

Lesson 11.2

1. 75
2. 2605
3. 26.666
4. 4,530
5. 176
6. 37.5
7. 649.231
8. 4,000
9. 2,977.273
10. 633.33
11. 17.5
12. 2,018.182

Lesson 11.3

1. .5
2. .064
3. .5893
4. .0395
5. .4494
6. .102
7. .00198
8. .0008
9. 10 Boxes
10. No, only 16.

Answers

Lesson 11.4

1. $0.45
2. $2.50
3. $5.59
4. $34.94
5. $90.92
6. $8.54
7. $78.90
8. $91.10
9. $3.20
10. $2.10
11. $96.30
12. $2.10
13. $424.00
14. $8.50
15. $56.20
16. $20.10
17. $2.70
18. $2.70
19. $3.40
20. $8.10

Lesson 11.5

1. 15
2. 3
3. 1
4. 3
5. 2
6. 10
7. 5
8. 2
9. 5
10. 12
11. 12
12. 4
13. 2
14. 20
15. 5
16. 12
17. 20
18. 20
19. 15
20. 8

Lesson 12.1

1. $.45, \frac{45}{100}$ or $\frac{9}{20}$
1. $.35, \frac{35}{100}$ or $\frac{7}{20}$
2. $.43, \frac{43}{100}$
3. $.1, \frac{10}{100}$ or $\frac{1}{10}$
4. $.87, \frac{87}{100}$
5. $.02, \frac{2}{100}$ or $\frac{1}{50}$
6. $.59, \frac{59}{100}$
7. $.001, \frac{1}{1000}$
8. $.0045, \frac{45}{10000}$ or $\frac{9}{2000}$
9. 76%
10. Each piece is equal to .1 or $\frac{1}{10}$ of the cake

Lesson 12.2

1. $\frac{7}{20}$
2. $\frac{47}{100}$
3. $\frac{1}{4}$
4. $\frac{3}{50}$
5. $\frac{91}{100}$
6. $\frac{523}{1000}$
7. $\frac{205}{10000}$ or $\frac{41}{2000}$
8. $\frac{17}{100}$
9. $\frac{495}{1000}$ or $\frac{99}{200}$
10. $\frac{1}{1000}$
11. 62.5%
12. 11.11%
13. 93.75%
14. 23.08%
15. 10%
16. 1.5%
17. .17%
18. 71.43%
19. 45.4%
20. .25%

Lesson 12.3

1. .1
2. .67
3. .0002
4. .964
5. .5532
6. 11.1001
7. .2346
8. .0008
9. .34
10. 10.03
11. 3%
12. 102%
13. .27%
14. 2.5%
15. 10001%
16. 14.5%
17. 1.01%
18. 12.5%
19. 8.25%
20. .9%

Lesson 12.4

1. $\frac{7}{120}$
2. $\frac{33}{175}$
3. $\frac{1}{16}$
4. $\frac{78}{125}$
5. $\frac{4}{150}$ or $\frac{2}{75}$
6. $\frac{6}{25}$
7. $\frac{111}{1300}$
8. $\frac{51}{800}$
9. $\frac{44}{225}$
10. $\frac{3}{170}$
11. 12.12%
12. 3.36%
13. 56.81%
14. 44%
15. 11.01%
16. 35.08%
17. 84.38%
18. 9.17%
19. 4.04%
20. .006%

Lesson 13.1

1. 8
2. 25
3. 1728
4. 64
5. 144
6. 6.25
7. 1000
8. 2401
9. 1.44
10. 625
11. 243
12. .0001
13. 128
14. .000125
15. 100,000
16. 1.21
17. 343
18. 625
19. 27,000
20. .000000008
21. 36
22. Take the $13.00, the other way adds up to $10.20

Lesson 13.2

1. 1.25×10^2
2. 7.453×10^3
3. 2.54×10^{-2}
4. 3.7×10^1
5. 4.57×10^{-3}
6. 1.222333×10^6
7. 8.98×10^2
8. 4.532×10^1
9. 1.90325×10^2
10. 1.3023×10^4
11. 5.567×10^0
12. 7.2354×10^1
13. 4.77777×10^3
14. 2.002×10^{-2}
15. 2.33323×10^2
16. 5.672×10^3

Answers

Lesson 14.1

1. 24
2. 74
3. 99
4. 3
5. −48
6. 81
7. 4
8. 28
9. −56

Lesson 14.2

1. Commutative Property of Multiplication
2. Commutative Property of Addition
3. Associative Property of Addition
4. Commutative Property of Multiplication
5. Associative Property of Multiplication
6. Commutative Property of Multiplication
7. Associative Property of Addition
8. Commutative Property of Multiplication
9. Commutative Property of Addition
10. Associative Property of Multiplication
11. Commutative Property of Addition
12. Commutative Property of Multiplication

Lesson 14.3

1. Identity of Addition
2. Distributive Property of Multiplication over Addition
3. Identity of Addition
4. Distributive Property of Multiplication over Addition
5. Identity of Multiplication
6. Identity of Addition
7. Distributive Property of Multiplication over Addition
8. Distributive Property of Division
9. Identity of Addition
10. Distributive Property of Multiplication over Addition
11. Identity of Addition
12. Distributive Property of Multiplication over Subtraction

Lesson 14.4

1. Equality Property of Multiplication
2. Equality Property of Division not by zero
3. Zero Property of Multiplication
4. Zero Property of Multiplication
5. Equality Property of Addition
6. Zero Property of Multiplication
7. Equality Property of Subtraction
8. Equality Property of Multiplication
9. Yes
10. Yes
11. No
12. Yes
13. Yes

Lesson 15.1

1. A number divided by six
2. A number plus four
3. A number multiplied by two plus ten
4. Five times a number minus five
5. A number less five, divided by thirty-three
6. The sum of three times a number plus four, times ten
7. Two times a number less three
8. A number minus twenty-two, times fourteen
9. Twenty-two minus three, times a number, plus two
10. Ten times a number minus three times the same number
11. Nine times a number divided by ten times the same number minus two
12. One-half of a number plus one fourth of the same number

Lesson 15.2

1. $w = 7$
2. $4 = q$
3. $y = 32$
4. $3 = e$
5. $s = 33$
6. $d = 15$
7. $z = 15$
8. $18 = r$
9. $m = 9$
10. $t = 18$
11. $15 = g$
12. $2 = f$
13. $r = 26$
14. $24 = u$
15. $r = 23$
16. $v = 86$

Lesson 15.3

1. $x = 3$
2. $m = 4$
3. $b = 11$
4. $p = 38$
5. $y = 343$
6. $u = 4$

Lesson 16.1

1. 0
2. 0
3. −1
4. 0
5. 3
6. 3
7. 0
8. −12
9. −3
10. 0
11. To the right of −6.2
12. Less than −4.0

Lesson 16.2

1. 8
2. −6
3. −10
4. 22
5. 102
6. 42
7. −17
8. 15
9. 1
10. 17
11. −1
12. 78
13. 16
14. −16
15. −1
16. 4
17. −24
18. 2

Answers

Lesson 16.3

1. A(1,2), B(3,−3),
   C(−5,−5), D(5,5),
   E(4,-5), F(1,1), G(−1,1),
   H(−4,4), I(8,8), J(−5,6)

2.
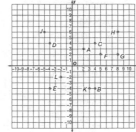

Lesson 17.1

1. 42 inches
2. 10,560 feet
3. $1\frac{1}{12}$ yards
4. 26,400 feet
5. 6.5 feet
6. 5.68 miles
7. $31\frac{1}{2}$ feet
8. 459,360 inches
9. 135 inches
10. 220,000 yards
11. .014 miles
12. 864 inches
13. 735 feet
14. .16 miles
15. .03 miles
16. 324,000 inches

Lesson 17.2

1. 8 pints
2. 92 quarts
3. $13\frac{1}{2}$ gallons
4. $1\frac{7}{8}$ gallons
5. 250 quarts
6. 500 cups
7. 456 pints
8. 84 cups
9. 4 gallons
10. 44 quarts
11. $62\frac{1}{2}$ pints
12. 250 cups
13. 308 quarts
14. $2\frac{3}{4}$ gallons
15. 64 gallons
16. 32 gallons

Lesson 17.3

1. 160 oz
2. 30,400 lb
3. 448,000 oz
4. $7\frac{13}{16}$ lb
5. 468 lb
6. $\frac{1}{2000}$ ton
7. 28,544 oz
8. $\frac{7}{8}$ lb
9. 64,000 lb
10. .073 ton
11. 723.2 oz
12. $1\frac{7}{8}$ tons
13. $\frac{1}{8}$ ton
14. 7,000 lb
15. 1,500 lb
16. $212\frac{1}{2}$ lb

Lesson 17.4

1. 8 inches
2. 12 feet
3. The square whose perimeter is 28 feet. The rectangle's perimeter is 26 feet.
4. 120 feet
5. The square's perimeter is 56 feet. The triangle's perimeter is 30 feet.
6. 19 in.
7. 600 feet
8. 1,300 feet

Lesson 17.5

1. 16 square feet
2. 24 square feet
3. 108 square feet
4. 51 square feet
5. 200 square feet
6. $312\frac{1}{2}$ square feet
7. 84 square feet
8. The square with sides of 14 ft. 187.5 square feet (triangle) vs. 196 square feet (square)

Lesson 17.6

1. 6600 cu yd
2. 840 cubic inches
3. 125 cu ft
4. 240 lb
5. 352 cubic feet
6. 216 cubic yards

Lesson 17.7

1. 86,400 seconds
2. 840 hours
3. 525,600 minutes
4. $\frac{1}{2}$ days
5. 364 days
6. 3,060 minutes
7. $3\frac{3}{7}$ weeks
8. 20 decades
9. 30 centuries
10. 60,480 minutes
11. 1,209,600 seconds
12. $\frac{3}{4}$ hours
13. $11.42 per hour
14. $108,000
15. 262,800 hours
16. 72 years old

Lesson 17.8

1. 0° C
2. 212° F
3. −100.6° C
4. 32° F
5. 37.8° C
6. 22.2° C
7. 89.6° F
8. 413.6° F
9. 4.4° C
10. 48.9° C
11. 122° F
12. 10° C
13. 41° F
14. −23.3° C
15. 14° F
16. −22° F

Lesson 18.1

1. 2.35 m
2. 4.235 m
3. 570,000 cm
4. 625 million mm
5. 2.65 m
6. 160,000 cm
7. .055 m
8. 3870 mm
9. 5050 m
10. 20,020,000 cm
11. .004 km
12. 2510 cm
13. 45,250 mm
14. 11,000 m
15. 33.363 m
16. .057 km

Answers

Lesson 18.2
1. 1100 mL
2. .7 kL
3. 560 mL
4. 35000 mL
5. 3,000,000 mL
6. .021 L
7. .000457 kL
8. 77.077 L
9. 1035 L
10. .041041 kL
11. 3675 L
12. 38.5 kL
13. 23.00023 L
14. 40977 mL
15. 120 cups (250 mL cups)
16. 175 L
17. 20 bottles
18. 100,000 kL

Lesson 18.3
1. .1 kg
2. 15,000,000 mg
3. .55 kg
4. 5.6 g
5. 1,100,000 mg
6. .1 g
7. 400.3 g
8. 320,000 cg
9. 870 g
10. 9.767 kg
11. 44.8 g
12. 3.3011 kg
13. 2199.66 g
14. 2960 g
15. 1.001001 kg
16. 14.835 g
17. 4210 cg
18. 3.535 kg
19. 97.9 kg
20. 33.363 g

Lesson 18.4
1. 20 m
2. 29.7 sq km
3. 8 cubic meters
4. 14,400 sq cm
5. 4.6656×10^{10} cubic meters
6. 99 square meters
7. 120 cubic meters
8. .06 cubic kilometers
9. 4 kilometers south; 18 kilometers total
10. 405 cubic meters
11. 40 square meters
12. 208 cubic kilometers
13. 25,000 meters
14. 28 square meters
15. 40 square meters
16. 24 truckloads

Lesson 19.1
1. .914 meters
2. 1.893 liters
3. $\frac{1}{2}$ liter soda bottle
4. 90.8 kg
5. 3.218 kilometers
6. The 100 meter dash
7. 400 liters
8. .5 kilogram steak
9. 1814.36 kilograms
10. 2 meters

Lesson 19.2
1. 2 liter bottle
2. 78.74 inches
3. 201 pounds
4. 62.1 miles per hour
5. 16.5 tons
6. 109.36 yards
7. No, $5.00/gal vs $6.63/gal
8. 7.392 quarts
9. 15 millimeters
10. A $\frac{1}{2}$ pound of steak

Lesson 20.1
1. $\overline{CD}$
2. Point M
3. $\overline{XT}$, $\overline{TX}$
4. No, the line does not continue beyond the points
5. Point C
6. Yes. The lines goes infinitely in both directions.

Lesson 20.2
1. $\overline{AB}$, $\overline{BC}$, $\overline{CD}$, $\overline{DA}$, $\overline{AE}$, $\overline{EB}$, $\overline{EC}$, $\overline{ED}$, $\overline{AC}$, $\overline{BD}$, $\overline{AD}$, $\overline{BE}$, $\overline{EA}$, $\overline{CE}$, $\overline{BA}$, $\overline{CB}$, $\overline{DC}$, $\overline{DE}$, $\overline{CA}$, $\overline{DB}$
2. 20 line segments
3. $\overrightarrow{DF}$, $\overrightarrow{DE}$, $\overrightarrow{BF}$, $\overrightarrow{GF}$, $\overrightarrow{AE}$, $\overrightarrow{LE}$
4. $\overrightarrow{NM}$, $\overrightarrow{NC}$, $\overrightarrow{NB}$, $\overrightarrow{AN}$, $\overrightarrow{LB}$

Lesson 21.1
1. Acute
2. Acute
3. Right
4. Obtuse
5. Acute
6. 41 degrees
7. 45 degrees
8. No
9. Angles A,C,F; angles A,E,F; angles A,C,E; angle A,B,F; angles B,C,F; angles B,E,F; angles C,E,F; angles A,B,E
10. No, the angles do not measure 90 degrees

Lesson 21.2
1. Yes, the sum of their measures is 180 degrees.
2. Yes, the sum of their measures is 90 degrees.
3. Yes, they form a straight line.
4. Cannot tell, there is not enough information.
5. Yes, they form a right angle.
6. ∠AOD, ∠DOB; Yes, they form a straight line.
7. Yes they are. 32° + 58° = 90°
8. 60 degree angle
9. ∠1 and ∠3; ∠2 and ∠4; ∠6 and ∠8; ∠5 and ∠7
10. ∠1 and ∠3; ∠2 and ∠4; ∠5 and ∠2; ∠3 and ∠2; ∠1 and ∠4; ∠5 and ∠1;
11. ∠1 and ∠3; ∠2 and ∠4;
12. Supplementary
13. ∠CBE and ∠ABD; ∠CBA and ∠DBE
14. ∠ACD and ∠DCB; Yes, they form a right angle.

Lesson 22.1
1. Acute
2. Right
3. Obtuse
4. Equilateral
5. Isosceles
6. Scalene

Lesson 22.2
1. Square
2. Kite
3. Rectangle
4. Rectangle
5. Trapezoid
6. Square
7. Trapezoid
8. Kite
9. Rhombus

Lesson 22.3

1. Hexagon
2. Pentagon
3. Heptagon
4. Octagon
5. Hexagon
6. Pentagon
7. Octagon
8. Hexagon
9. Cannot tell, do not know length of sides.
10. No

Lesson 22.4

1. 5.5 cm
2. $\overline{AB}$
3. $\overline{OB}$, $\overline{OA}$
4. $\overline{AB}$, $\overline{BC}$, $\overline{CD}$, $\overline{DE}$, $\overline{EA}$, $\overline{BA}$, $\overline{CB}$, $\overline{ED}$, $\overline{AE}$, $\overline{DC}$
5. $\overline{BA}$ and $\overline{CD}$ are chords
6. $\overline{BC}$

Lesson 22.4 (cont.)

1. 94.2 inches
2. 78.5 sq cm
3. Area = 28.26 square feet, Circumference 18.84 feet
4. Area = 7.065 square yards, Circumference = 9.42 yards
5. Area = 254.3 square inches, Circumference = 56.52 inches
6. $\overline{PQ}$, $\overline{AB}$

Lesson 22.5

1. 5 faces
2. 6 faces
3. Circle
4. 8 faces
5. 6 edges
6. 8 faces
7. 8 vertices
8. 1 vertex
9. 18 edges
10. 8 vertices, 12 edges

Lesson 23.1

1. Apples
2. Red
3. Car
4. May
5. Ontario
6. 7

Lesson 23.2

1. 1996 and 1997
2. 50
3. Monday and Friday
4. Day 2 and Day 3
5. Wednesday and Sunday, 65 kilos
6. Overall increase from January to March with two dips and a large increase from February to March

Lesson 23.3

1. As the price goes down the demand for chocolate increases
2. The more TV you watch the lower the grades in Math and Reading
3. The temperature in Hawaii is pretty steady throughout the year, while the temperature in Wisconsin rises and falls to coincide with the seasons of spring, summer, fall and winter.
4. They rose in the United States and remained flat or steady in Europe.
5. It takes longer to sell a condominium than a single family home and that difference is increasing.
6. From August to September Kate's sales rose while Harry's sales fell.
7. Lisa's book collection grew faster than her CD collection.

Lesson 23.4

1. Marketing
2. People shifted the way they communicated from paper to electronic.
3. Yes, 67% vs 33%
4. No
5. Yes
6. Over 25 years

Lesson 24.1

1. 21
2. 4.5
3. 5
4. 6
5. 40
6. 42.9
7. $20
8. The average would go higher.

Lesson 24.2

1. 19, 22, 25, 26, 30, 52, 53, 55, 62
   Range = 43
2.
   ```
   5 | 5
   6 |
   7 | 5 7 9
   8 | 2 3 4 8 9
   9 | 0 5
   ```

Lesson 24.3

1. 78
2. 71 and 91
3. 15
4. 30
5. 16
6. Range: 5, Median: 8
7. 14
8. They are equal in range.
9. Half the class weighs more than him and half the class weighs less than him.
10. .94

Lesson 24.4

1. 9
2. 8
3.
4. One
5. 8
6.

Lesson 24.5

1. 30
2. 76
3. 19
4. 92

Lesson 24.6

1. $\frac{15}{35}$ or $\frac{3}{7}$
2. $\frac{12}{40}$ or $\frac{3}{10}$
3. $\frac{3}{12}$ or $\frac{1}{4}$
4. $\frac{6}{7}$
5. $\frac{6}{18}$ or $\frac{1}{3}$
6. $\frac{3}{20}$

Answers

Pretest

1. 300,635
2. 5,000
3. 912
4. 825
5. 2574
6. 3652
7. $\frac{11}{2}, 5\frac{1}{2}$
8. $76.90
9. $76.98
10. $6.01
11. $100.50
12. 9.3 in.
13. 25 R1
14. 18 R13
15. 4 R13
16. 13 R2
17. 51.75 mL of blue, 40.35 mL of yellow and 92.1 mL of paint
18. 72
19. .3 and $\frac{3}{10}$
20. $8\frac{17}{20}$
21. .0001, .0016, .019, .0234, .05, .0978, .11, .45, .8, 1.076
22. $7\frac{7}{12}$, No, No
23. Tuesday, Thursday
24. Sydney, August
25. Cone
26. $\frac{1}{2}$
27. C, B, A
28. 22
29. 1.6784830043 $\times$ 10^6
30. $114
31. E, D, C
32. 128
33. 5.01
34. $\frac{4}{35}$
35. 34
36. $\frac{2}{3}$
37. 18 L of water, 8 lb trail mix
38. About 2 hours
39. 7.875
40. $\frac{6}{5}$ or $1\frac{1}{5}$
41. 12 cups of flour, 6 cups of water
42. 20%
43. .3, $\frac{3}{10}$
44. Perimeter 14 cm, Area 12 sq cm
45. 100 in., 254 cm

Posttest

1. 300,252
2. 1000
3. 459
4. 504
5. 5832
6. 896
7. $\frac{13}{2}$
8. $75.25
9. $83.69
10. $10.50
11. $166.87
12. 5.2 inches
13. 20 R11
14. 18
15. 5 R3
16. 13 R4
17. 95 mL of black paint, 36.8 mL of white paint, 131.8 mL of grey paint
18. 60
19. .16, $\frac{4}{25}$
20. 12.075 m
21. .0003, .0019, .0245, .029, .06, .0925, .21, .75, .9, 3.084
22. 86.737 kg, No
23. Thursday, Wednesday,
24. Buenos Aires, August
25. Cylinder
26. penny $\frac{5}{9}$ or .56, dime $\frac{1}{6}$ or .167, nickel $\frac{5}{18}$ or .28
27. C, B, A
28. 24
29. 2.23458360071 x 10^6
30. $21.00
31. E,D,C
32. 112
33. 6.01
34. $\frac{22}{217}$
35. 67.5
36. $\frac{2}{3}$
37. 21 L of water, 8.75 pounds of trail mix
38. 1.55 hours
39. 9.375
40. $\frac{18}{5}$
41. $14\frac{2}{3}$ cups of sugar, $\frac{4}{3}$ (or $1\frac{1}{3}$) cups of chocolate chips
42. 24%
43. .15, $\frac{3}{20}$
44. Perimeter 24 cm, Area 35 sq cm
45. 157.5 in., 645.16 centimeters

Unit Test Lesson 1–3

1. 311
2. 505
3. 1,573
4. 4,906
5. 1,212
6. 652,576
7. 838
8. 62
9. 1,219
10. 6,395
11. 4,889
12. 379
13. 21,022
14. 53,931
15. 66,711
16. 151,262
17. 66,587
18. 89,853
19. 193
20. 1,389
21. 28,716,878
22. 11,716
23. 37,866
24. 6,984
25. 612
26. 688
27. 3,820
28. 1,012
29. 3,870
30. 6,055
31. 8 R6
32. 10 R3
33. 14 R1
34. 12 R42
35. 25 R1
36. 4 R24
37. 58,092
38. 37,638
39. 266,140
40. 66,521,052
41. 2,176,270
42. 69,164,605
43. 21
44. 45 R8
45. 6 R9
46. 12 R42
47. 1207 R4
48. 782 R6
49. 1040 students
50. 15 classes, 18 classes, 13 classes
51. 511 stamps
52. About 1000 pages, 799 pages exactly
53. one thousand six hundred twenty two
54. (7 × 1,000,000) + (4 × 100,000) + (5 × 10,000) + (6 × 1,000) + (9 × 100) + (3 × 10) + (2 × 1)

Answers

55. 274,943,496;
305,444,446;
$(3 \times 100,000,000) +$
$(5 \times 1,000,000) +$
$(4 \times 100,000) +$
$(4 \times 10,000) +$
$(4 \times 1,000) + (4 \times 100)$
$+ (4 \times 10) + (6 \times 1)$

Unit Test Lesson 4–7

1. $2\frac{1}{7}$
2. $4\frac{3}{5}$
3. 5
4. $9\frac{5}{34}$
5. $\frac{62}{7}$
6. $\frac{130}{9}$
7. $\frac{86}{23}$
8. $\frac{131}{31}$
9. 1
10. $\frac{5}{43}$
11. $1\frac{1}{7}$
12. $\frac{47}{59}$
13. $\frac{11}{47}$
14. $\frac{6}{7}$
15. $\frac{47}{94}$ or $\frac{1}{2}$
16. $\frac{56}{73}$
17. $1\frac{1}{7}$
18. $1\frac{39}{77}$
19. $1\frac{8}{35}$
20. $\frac{106}{725}$
21. $\frac{53}{99}$
22. $\frac{13}{57}$
23. $\frac{1}{78}$
24. $\frac{305}{323}$

25. $1\frac{20}{23}$
26. $26\frac{1}{21}$
27. $24\frac{11}{29}$
28. $15\frac{9}{28}$
29. $22\frac{1}{2}$
30. 33
31. 135
32. $6\frac{6}{23}$
33. $2\frac{26}{27}$
34. $2\frac{4}{7}$
35. $11\frac{19}{29}$
36. $12\frac{14}{47}$
37. $\frac{1}{54}$
38. $\frac{4}{27}$
39. $\frac{1}{21}$
40. $10\frac{1}{2}$
41. 40
42. 81
43. $1\frac{19}{56}$
44. $\frac{16}{49}$
45. $\frac{1}{6}$
46. $\frac{32}{105}$
47. $2\frac{13}{19}$
48. $7\frac{1}{11}$
49. $\frac{1}{8}$ of a pizza
50. 1 red for every 5 black cars
51. No
52. No
53. No
54. Yes
55. $58\frac{1}{2}$ miles

56. 7 batches
57. 3 pints
58. Yes, he will
59. 4 quarts

Unit Test Lesson 8–12

1. Hundredths
2. Ten thousands
3. Ten thousandths
4. Hundred thousands
5. 567,893.55
6. 500,000
7. $\frac{17}{20}$
8. $\frac{5}{8}$
9. $\frac{3}{50}$
10. $\frac{3}{8}$
11. .8
12. .2667
13. .875
14. 4.125
15. .89, .765, .76, .45, .432, .43, .226, .22
16. .657, .243, .2043, .117, .087, .0657, .0605, .033, .017
17. .92817
18. .471816
19. 1.58932
20. 3.2961
21. .192611
22. .69266
23. 18.62
24. 2.7297
25. 1107.675
26. 13.095
27. .52822
28. .28032
29. .5036248
30. $39.36
31. .3231
32. .669
33. 1.6693
34. 3.004
35. 21.8

36. .73288
37. 2.002
38. 496
39. $104.25
40. $\frac{9}{50}$
41. 96
42. 180%
43. 80%
44. 14%
45. 72%
46. .13915
47. .39864

Unit Test Lesson 13–16

1. $2^4 + 3^3 = 43$
2. $4^4 - 5^3 = 131$
3. $2^6 + 6^2 - 5^2 = 75$
4. 3.45698401×10^6
5. 8.6941×10^3
6. 9.45×10^{-3}
7. 1.094659041×10^9
8. 6.356×10^1
9. 79
10. 32
11. 73
12. 59
13. Commutative Property of Addition
14. Distributive Property of Multiplication over Addition
15. Associative Property of Addition
16. Multiplication Identity Property of 1
17. Zero Identity of Addition
18. Distributive Property of Multiplication over Subtraction
19. Commutative Property of Multiplication
20. Zero Property of Addition and Multiplication
21. Associative Property of Multiplication

Answers

22. $x = 3$
23. $x = 17$
24. $x = 4$
25. $x = 60$
26. $x = 2$
27. $x = 6$
28. $x = 7$
29. $x = 8$
30. $x = 8$
31. $x = 80$
32. $x = 70$
33. $x = 45$
34. A
35. D
36. B
37. C
38. (2,3)
39. (3,4)
40. (−3,4)
41. (3,−4)
42. (−3,−4)
43. (6,7)
44. (−4,5)
45. (−5,−5)
46.

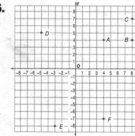

Unit Test Lessons 17–19

1. 93 feet
2. 44 gallon containers
3. The first plant; the third plant
4. $146\frac{1}{4}$ ft
5. 240 sq ft
6. 6 sq ft
7. 4.5 cu ft
8. 294 mi; 17,640 mi; 423,360 mi
9. 82 minutes or 1.36 hours; 17.6 times a day; 123 times per week; 6,424 times per year
10. 369 cm higher
11. 60,750 sq cm
12. 6.19 L
13. 18 sq cm
14. 242 m
15. 366.85 cubic meters
16. 193 cm
17. 17.2 gallons
18. 1620 sq ft; 180 sq yds; 150 sq meters
19. 37° C
20. 68° − 72° F
21. 120 cubic inches
22. 270 cubic inches
23. 4920 ft; 360 feet; 110 meters
24. $4\frac{1}{2}$ hours

Unit Test Lesson 20–22

1. Obtuse
2. Right
3. Acute
4. Acute
5. Obtuse
6. Neither; measure of ∠DAC + measure of ∠CAB = 90°
7. Supplementary; measure of ∠DAC + measure of ∠CAB = 180°
8. Complementary; measure of ∠DAC + measure of ∠CAB < 90°
9. Isosceles
10. Scalene
11. Equilateral
12. Scalene
13. Equilateral
14. Scalene
15. Obtuse
16. Obtuse
17. Right
18. Right
19. Acute
20. Acute
21. Obtuse
22. Right
23. Acute
24. Acute
25. Acute
26. Obtuse
27. Rectangle
28. Rhombus
29. Trapezoid
30. Kite
31. A
32. $\overline{BD}$, $\overline{DC}$, $\overline{CB}$
33. $\overline{FG}$
34. $\overline{AG}$, $\overline{AF}$, $\overline{AD}$
35. cube, square, 6, 12, 8

36. rectangular prism, rectangle, 6, 12, 8
37. rectangular pyramid, rectangle, 5, 8, 5
38. triangular prism, rectangle, 5, 9, 6
39. triangular pyramid, triangle, 4, 6, 4
40. cone, circle, 2, 0, 1
41. cylinder, circle, 3, 0, 0

Unit Test Lesson 23–24

1. Sunday; Wednesday and Friday; 20
2. May; 110; March
3. 17, Canada
4. Cereal, Yes, 30% versus 28% so 2%
5. 8.6, 8.5, 10
6. 4 | 5 6 9
   5 | 5 6 6 9 9
   6 | 0 3 4 5 5 5
   7 | 1 1 2 6 8
   8 | 1
7.

   range = 36
   median = 63.5
8.

   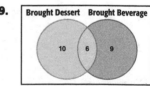

   black stone first pick $\frac{2}{3}$, white stone first pick $\frac{1}{3}$
9.

Brought Dessert		Brought Beverage
10	6	9

   6 brought both; 36%
10. $\frac{9}{16}$; $\frac{15}{16}$
11. 60%; 5%; 75%